Wake Up
to your
Dreams

Wake Up
to your
Dreams

*A Practical Self-help Guide
to Interpretation*

Linda Sheppard
B.A. Psych

BLANDFORD

A BLANDFORD BOOK
First published in the UK 1994 by Blandford
A Cassell imprint
Villiers House
41–47 Strand, London WC2N 5JE

Distributed in the United States by Sterling Publishing Co., Inc.
387 Park Avenue South, New York, NY 10016–8810

Distributed in Australia by Capricorn Link (Australia) Pty Ltd
2/13 Carrington Road, Castle Hill, NSW 2154

British Library Cataloguing-in-Publication Data
A catalogue entry for this title is available from the British Library

ISBN 0–7137–2448–X

Typeset by Method Limited, Epping, Essex, UK

Printed and bound in Finland by Werner Söderström Oy

CONTENTS

To all dream-workers

Acknowledgements

I WOULD LIKE TO THANK all my clients, past and present, for their contributions to my book and to my growth and understanding. I also thank my friends and clients for nagging me to finish it and Peter in particular for adding his support and suggestions. A big thank you to Stuart Booth, the commissioning editor at Cassell, for taking me on board and to all the staff at Cassell who have demonstrated a very sensitive and caring attitude towards producing the finished manuscript. Finally, I would like to acknowledge all the therapists and teachers, too many to mention, who have guided me through the maze of my own dreams over the years, and also the enormous contribution that the works of Carl Gustav Jung have made to our understanding of dreams and their powers of transformation.

Preface

MORE AND MORE people today are becoming interested in those wonderful inner movie shows that we call dreams. Often a person will wake up with strange and bewildering images and landscapes still fresh in his or her mind. Many such images will remain firmly lodged there for days, months and even for years, so vivid are their colours, stories and emotional content. Yet how much attention do we pay to them?

This book takes a look at the part that dreams play in our physical, emotional and psychological growth. Dreams are essentially practical and instructive, and this book will explore ways of understanding and interpreting their messages, for in attending to our dreams we will be taking a step towards greater health and awareness.

The first part of the book deals with the physiological aspect of sleep patterns, the way in which dreams have been used and interpreted throughout history, and the use of dreams in some twentieth-century primitive societies. The second part gives some ideas about recording, interpreting and using your dreams as an aid to self-awareness. The techniques in this book can be used by one person alone, in conjunction with a friend, or with a group. Case histories of clients from my own practice have been included, although the names of individuals have been changed to protect their identity.

I would like to thank all those who have allowed me to share their inner journeys with them and whose dreams have provided me with such inspiration.

Linda Sheppard

Introduction

IN MY WORK as a psychotherapist I have been privileged to share and explore the dreams of many people during the course of their therapy. Many of these people were initially very sceptical about the relevance or significance of their dreams to their everyday lives or development. However, as we ventured into these subconscious landscapes together, trusting our intuitive nature to play with associations and unlock the symbols to reveal their hidden wisdom, clients joined with me in joy and amazement at the insight and humour that they were able to access.

Like most people, I had always been aware of my dreams but had never given them a great deal of attention apart from recounting them occasionally to friends, especially if they were bizarre or amusing. However, my interest grew in earnest when, in my early twenties, I had a series of transformative dreams that possessed a vividness and energy that I can still access today whenever I recall them. At the time I did not know how they were affecting me, except that afterwards I felt the need to make some dramatic changes in my life.

These were the catalysts for my own inner journey, which has been an on-going process, through psychotherapy and self-development, ever since. When I was first helped to explore my own dreams I can remember what a relief and fascination it was to be shown that dream analysis was an age-old path to self-knowledge and that dreams were a very important way of connecting to a deeper sense of knowing and wisdom. I had proof for myself that they were not to be dismissed as a meaningless jumble of images that were the result of the mind having a nightly purge – a belief prevalent among many 'authorities' at the time.

When I subsequently went on to study psychology at university,

I was unable to find any real investigation or understanding of the psyche about which this science claimed to teach. During the late seventies, psychology students spent a good deal of their time studying the behaviour of rats in mazes and feeding statistics into computers. Psychology was still defined by psychologists as 'the science of nature, function and phenomena of the human mind', but this was a mind based on purely physiological mechanics.

What was missing was that aspect of the 'psyche' that connects us with our spiritual or transpersonal self. Such an energy as this could not (and maybe should not) be measured by clinical, scientific means because its very nature is mercurial, numinous and creative. However, it can be measured by us all as individuals if we allow ourself to communicate with it through its own language, the language of symbols and imagery, and then observe how we can change and grow through utilizing and integrating its wisdom. Dreams provide a wonderful vehicle for this language.

Throughout this book I refer to the word 'psyche' as if it is an intelligence in its own right, something which is wanting to reveal itself to us. I make no apologies for this, since my own experience has shown me that the more I can trust this aspect of my being as a teacher or guide, even if it shows me things that seem to fly in the face of logic, the more I am rewarded with insight and empowerment. In essence, however, the psyche is not a separate entity but very much a natural part of our consciousness. Some people call it the 'Higher Self' or the 'still, small voice' – the latter suggesting, appropriately, that we need to quieten our questioning, restless, rationalizing minds in order to communicate with our psyche or spiritual nature. Certainly we need to find a new way of listening and observing, thus heightening our awareness and sensitivity.

Sadly, Western culture and educational systems do not teach or encourage such awareness; as a result it can sometimes feel like a struggle, initially at least, to re-tune ourselves to this inner guidance. We are, after all, predominantly left-hemisphere creatures: that is, we are adept at the so-called rational activities of language, numbers and and analytical thought that are controlled by the left hemisphere of the brain. It was the American psychologist Robert Ornstein who suggested this functional difference between the two hemispheres of the brain and, although the relationship between them is still not clear, it is apparently the right hemisphere that is concerned with our imagination and artistic instincts. These talents are relatively unacknowledged in our society today; it is therefore no wonder that we have to work so hard at re-entering this rich, imaginative world, as our resistance to it is very strong.

Now it is time for us to get the balance right and remember where our real wisdom lies. John Bradshaw, an American counsellor and theologian who has looked at many of the issues that lead to societal and personal breakdown in our modern age, wrote in *Bradshaw On: The Family* (Health Communications, Inc., 1988): 'We are spiritual beings on an earthly journey. Our spirituality makes up our beingness. We are the kind of spiritual beings who, in order to adequately be spirits, need a body. We are not earthly beings trying to get spiritual. We are *essentially spiritual.*' (My italics.)

Our dreams, with their quality of transcending time and space, enable us for a while at least to reconnect with our essential spirituality, which is subtle and fluid. They provide vital information about our multi-faceted wholeness and our infinite potential for growth and creativity. Honour your dreams!

PART I

The Dream World

CHAPTER I

The Dream
on the Machine

IF YOU ASK people today whether they dream or not, a fair proportion will say that they do not. They would be more correct if
they said that they do not remember what they have dreamt, because
most people will have had several dreams during the course of a
night's sleep, irrespective of whether or not they feel that dreams
have any significance or value. We are all natural dreamers.

Research using an electroencephalograph (EEG) machine, which
records the electrical activity in the brain, has shown that during an
average night's sleep there is a regular pattern of brain activity which
follows a cyclic rhythm. The first stage of this pattern is often called
'quiet sleep' because of the slow, regular, brain activity, known as
alpha rhythm, shown on the EEG machine. Breathing is slower, the
heart rate decreases, and body temperature and blood pressure fall. If
a person is awakened from slow-wave sleep he is usually groggy.
Dreams are seldom reported, but if they are, they are likely to be
simple and primitive in structure.

Next, the EEG shows a change to stage 2 sleep, during which the
brain waves recorded are slow, spindling, regular patterns or bursts of
higher frequencies. Sleep-walking or sleep-talking may occur in this
cycle. Several minutes later, the slow delta waves of stage 3 appear,
showing stronger electrical impulses from the brain. This is a prelude
to the deepest level of sleep, which is stage 4.

Stage 4 sleep produces large, slow waves on the EEG and it is very
difficult to awaken the sleeper at this time. It takes about 30–40 minutes to reach this point, and the sleeper may stay at this stage for

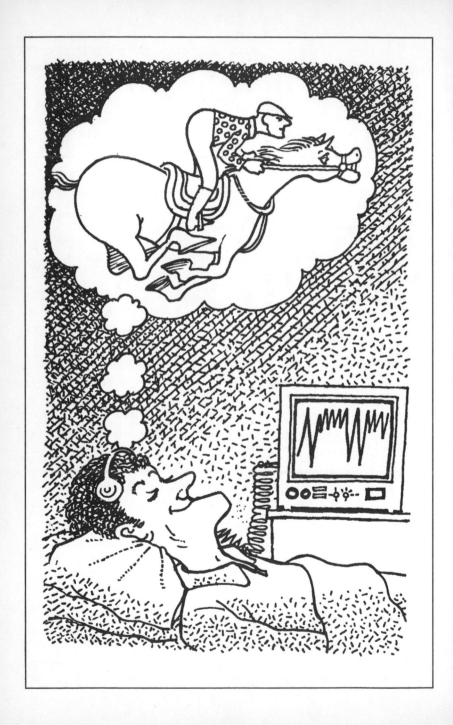

about 30 minutes in the first cycle. This stage 4 is followed by a re-ascent through the stages to stage 1, which can take about 70–80 minutes. However, this time stage 1 sleep is different. The EEG now shows saw-tooth theta waves, and the eyes begin to move and flicker under the closed eyelids as though the person is actually looking at something. Hence this stage has been called Rapid Eye Movement (REM) sleep, as opposed to the Non-Rapid Eye Movement (NREM) sleep of stage 1.

At this stage, also, there is convulsive twitching of the face and fingers and the breathing becomes irregular. There is a general muscular relaxation, particularly in the neck, and the heart rate and blood pressure decrease. At this time there can be penile erections in men and vaginal moistening in women. It is even harder to wake people up now, but if they are awoken at this stage they will generally be able to report vividly detailed dreams, especially as the cycles progress. After about 10 minutes the sleeper descends the scale of sleep again, but on re-ascent will then spend a longer time in stage 1, or dreaming, sleep – perhaps 20 minutes or so – before descending again.

Throughout the night this cyclic variation between NREM and REM sleep continues in 90-minute cycles, but with each re-ascent the interesting thing is that the sleeper spends more and more time in the REM dreaming stage. So an adult who sleeps about seven and a half hours each night generally spends one and a half to two hours in REM sleep: that is, about 25 per cent of the time (or four to six periods) is spent in stage 1 or dreaming sleep.

We all know that loss of sleep can make us feel very disoriented. Studies have shown that sleep loss over two to three days is highly stressful, leading to short attention span, hand tremors, visual distortions and hallucinations. There is an inability to concentrate, slurring of speech and immediate memory loss. Animals deprived of sleep for several days may fight and kill each other; humans can become psychotic and paranoid. It is particularly stressful to lose the dreaming stage of sleep. Both animals and humans show increasing behavioural disorganization with increasing REM sleep loss. There can be psychotic-like behaviour and some studies have discovered irritability and ravenous appetites. Experiments in which animals have been deprived of REM sleep have found increased motor activity and exploratory behaviour, plus hypersexuality. It is also worth noting that scientific experiments have confirmed that the abnormal behaviour of drug addicts and alcoholics may be connected with the suppression of normal REM sleep. This may be triggered by body chemicals with which the drugs or alcohol interfere.

Babies spend a long time in the stage of dreaming sleep, and yet senile and mentally handicapped people spend much less than the normal amount of time in this stage. This has led to a possible conclusion that the REM dream stage of sleep may be connected with the more evolved brain functions of thinking, remembering and learning. Indeed, if a sleeper is awakened every time she enters dream sleep, she begins to enter dream sleep more often. When finally allowed to sleep undisturbed, she stays in dream sleep for very long periods and enters straight into this stage as if in an effort to make up for lost time. Modern experimentation, therefore, has shown that dream sleep seems to serve a very important function in the overall balance of the health of humans and animals.

CHAPTER 2

Dreams Throughout Time

Throughout the ages, dreams have been respected for their valuable contribution to the process of living. Their sheer creativity, power and mystery were felt to be an important part of everyday life in many ancient civilizations. In Egypt, as far back as 2000 BC, special dream temples were built for the purposes of dream divination by priests, who were skilled in invoking and interpreting them.

The Egyptians and the Assyrians had dream books which dealt with positive and negative dreams, symbol and word associations and puns. They also felt that some dreams often depicted an opposite meaning: for example, to dream of death might mean that the dreamer would like a long life. This theory of the contrary meaning of certain dreams was later to be suggested by Sigmund Freud. Dreams were also valued as a means of curing illness. In Egypt, and later in Greece, special incubation temples existed where a sick or disturbed person would swallow drugs or herbal potions concocted to induce sleep and encourage dreams. Afterwards, the priest would interpret the meaning of the dreams and administer the cure prescribed therein. Temples in Greece were based on sacred sites, each with a respective god of healing; the most famous of these was Aesculapius, the god of medicine, whose symbol was the snake.

The prophetic element of dreams has long been a source of fascination. The early Jews, with their all-seeing god Yahweh, felt that all divine dreams were a direct link with God and were intended to lead the way to a fuller and more enlightened life. The Old

Testament of the Bible is full of dreams; special interpreters of dreams were sought by men of such rank as Nebuchadnezzar, as well as by ordinary people. Interpreters were sought with care, and the Bible warns people to beware of false prophets. In the Islamic culture, the Prophet Mohammed took great interest in his dreams and encouraged his disciples to share their dreams with him. Much of the Koran was said to be dictated to him in a dream.

The first notable compilation of dreams was undertaken in the second century AD by a Greek called Artemidorus. The book, called the *Oneirocrituca*, was reissued in 1644 in England, with great success. Artemidorus interpreted dreams according to the unique make-up of the dreamer, his name, occupation, status, health and so on. Although still believing that dreams were influenced by the gods, he was very practical in his approach to the interpretation. He was really heralding the approach of modern-day psychiatrists and psychoanalysts in that he was aware of the way dreams used puns and, more importantly, association to illustrate a point. In other words, a dream image would evoke a response via its relationship to other images in the conscious mind of the dreamer, thus revealing the dream's deeper meaning.

With the advent of Christianity dreams were again considered the messages of God, this time the Christian God, and dreams figured in the writings of many saints including St Clement and St Augustine. But in the fifth century it was St Jerome who, plagued by dreams that challenged his allegiance to Christianity, decided that dreams were of the devil and witchcraft. This led to a general condemnation of dreams by the Church over the next few centuries. Eventually, however, with the widespread proliferation of the printed word, the works of such scholars as Artemidorus surfaced again and interest in dream meanings was renewed. Dreaming was also introduced into poetry and literature, despite disapproval by the intellectuals and rationalists of the day. 'To sleep, perchance to dream,' wrote Shakespeare and later, in the nineteenth century, the American poet Edgar Allen Poe asked: 'Is all that we see or seem but a dream within a dream?'

CHAPTER 3

The Birth of Analysis

As the nineteenth century progressed, dreams were again challenged by an increasingly rationalist age. Scientific knowledge questioned superstition, myth and dream, but out of this came a new orientation: that dreams were not phenomena set apart from man and influenced by divine intervention, but a product of man's own psyche and a tool for personal instruction and self-knowledge. It was in Germany, where philosophers began to develop the concept of the unconscious, that the links between dreams and the personality began to be researched. Also, at about the same period in France, some pioneering work was being carried out by the psychologist Alfred Maury, who investigated the connection between external stimuli and dreams. For example, a pair of scissors being sharpened near him when he was asleep were experienced in his dream as the pealing of bells.

In England, the physiologist David Hartley was researching dreams as a reflection of memories of external stimuli which occurred during waking consciousness. He was also interested in what dreams could say about a person's health. Gradually, the stage was being set for the modern-day pioneer of analysis of the unconscious mind, Sigmund Freud.

It was 1900 when Freud published his book *The Interpretation of Dreams*. Far from considering dreams a random series of responses to external stimuli, Freud felt that they were a very ingenious method of expressing man's innermost needs and desires by disguising forbidden wishes in symbolic form. He spent the rest of his life trying to interpret the imagery of the unconscious. The scope of Freud's work is too wide to attempt to cover in this book; suffice it to say that he used a method called free association to find the underlying meaning of the dream imagery. In free association, a person is asked to talk about his dream images and the thoughts that these prompt in his mind until he reveals the unconscious motives behind the dream. According to Freud, the dreamer remembers certain images which make up the manifest dream content; after analysis the underlying meaning of the dream is slowly revealed, and this he called the latent content. Freud felt that dream symbols were used to disguise those thoughts, feelings and wish-fulfilments which would not be acceptable to the waking consciousness – erotic desires, for instance, or violent instinctual emotions. He said that most of these feelings could be traced back to childhood and to such primitive urges as the wish to commit incest or to murder the parent of the same sex because of childhood jealousy.

He was also rather fixed in his interpretation, believing that certain symbols always had the same meaning: for instance, 'there is no doubt that all weapons and tools are used as symbols for the male organ'. He also said that rooms always represented women, and the uterus might be represented by a cupboard or a carriage. Unfortunately this theory tended to neglect the unique relationship of meaning that each symbol has for each individual, and it also overlooked the wonderful richness of symbols which can open the dreamer to influences of the past, present or future. But it was really Freud's insistence that dreams were merely the disguised fulfilment of repressed desires, and his belief that the straightforward contents were of little significance, that caused a parting of the ways between him and many of his contemporaries. One such contemporary, a former admirer of Freud's teachings, was Carl Gustav Jung.

Jung too has made a great impact on dream analysis. In his attitude to dreams he diverged from Freud in a number of ways, but mainly he felt that Freud's theory was too restrictive. Jung suggested that dreams were more than mere receptacles for disguising suppressed wishes and fears. He felt that Freud focused too narrowly on instinctual desires and ignored the rest of the spectrum of man's experiences, such as his religious fantasies, memories and anticipations. In addition, instead of relying on free association to trace an image back to certain memories, Jung used a technique called amplification. Here, elements in the dream were taken at face value and explored, for example, on the level of sensation. This might then lead to a metaphysical meaning. For instance, if a person dreamed of holding a frog, Jung would ask that person to explore the feeling of holding the frog, its texture, weight and any memories or significance it might have in the dreamer's life.

Jung also introduced the theory of the collective unconscious, which was a form of race or primitive memory shared by all people. Within this deeper structure are facets of the human psyche such as the persona, the shadow, the anima, the animus and archetypes. These various facets will be discussed more fully later; suffice it to say here that Jung considerably widened and deepened the possibilities of dream interpretation and provided some very useful techniques for understanding and working with dream imagery.

Unlike Freud, Jung researched widely such areas of knowledge as mythology, alchemy and primitive cultures in order to obtain greater understanding of the richness of the psyche and symbolism. The concept of thinking, he discovered, was far more connected with the heart than with the head in most primitive societies; a great deal of their understanding of the world was gained through their well-developed intuitive sense and their access to the rich world of symbols, imagery and dreams.

CHAPTER 4

Shared Dreams

I N MANY PRIMITIVE societies today dreams are considered to be the language of the soul. Modern anthropologists have investigated and documented the ways dreams are used by these societies to understand and deal with everyday living.

The American Indians have always regarded their dreams with respect and see them as a vital part of the education and initiation of the young. The culture of the Australian aborigines is centred on the 'Dreamtime', which enables them to receive messages and instructions about day-to-day living. The Zulu people of southern Africa regard dreams as messages from their ancestors, while the Iroquois of North America see dreams as the language of the soul. They believe that dreams can be indications, albeit in coded form, of the dreamer's deepest and most secret wishes.

The Naskapi Indians, who live in the forests of the Labrador peninsula in Canada, rely upon their dreams for guidance and teaching. These simple people are hunters who live in isolated family groups and, because the groups are so far apart, have no evolved tribal customs or collective religious beliefs and ceremonies. The Naskapi hunter therefore has to rely on his own inner voices and unconscious revelations. In his basic view of life, the soul of man is simply an 'inner companion', whom the Naskapi refer to as the 'Great Man'. By listening to their dreams and trying to test out their meaning, the Naskapi feel they can enter into a deeper connection with the Great Man who will then send them more and better dreams. They honour their dreams and give permanent form to their content in tribal art; in return, the dreams give them instructions on how to deal with their inner world and the outer world of nature. They can, for instance, help the individual to foretell the weather and give him valuable guidance in his hunting, upon which the life of each family group depends.

Another society which understands the importance of dreams is that of the Senoi, in the central mountain range of Malaya. These people live more communal lives than the Naskapi Indians and are exceptional for their advanced level of psychological knowledge, social cooperation and creating thinking. They teach the art of dreaming to their children; every morning the father and his oldest sons analyse the dreams of the other children and encourage them to live these dreams to the full and to act upon them the following night in what is known as lucid or 'conscious' dreaming. This is a very advanced form of dreaming. If a child, for example, reports floating dreams or a dream of finding food, he is told that he must float somewhere in particular in his next dream and find something of value to his fellows or that he must share the food he is eating whilst in the dream. In this way, psychic and emotional energy created during the dream state is fully integrated into consciousness and is directed and organized accordingly.

An important factor to emerge from this exercise is that, in discussing their dreams openly, the children feel socially accepted. The act of being able to communicate their deepest psychic reactions to others for approval and criticism, and for these to be accepted, shows the children that they can depend on the deepest possible acceptance from the community. This factor alone is probably responsible for the feelings of goodwill that are prevalent in this tribe.

We in the West may, therefore, have lost something of great value by ignoring our dream life. After all, if we deny such instinctual aspects of ourselves as our dream life and inner psychic process, how can we ever fully understand and accept other people? In the words of the Delphic Oracle, 'Man, know thyself'. But we *can* all make a start by deciding to record whatever we remember of our dreams the next morning. In Part II of this book we will begin to map the psyche and its many aspects, and attempt to build up some way of understanding the meaning of a dream. All you need are a notebook, a pen and the willingness to learn and grow by respecting the dream process.

Dream Interpretation

CHAPTER 5

The Preliminaries

THE MOST ESSENTIAL pieces of equipment you will need to begin your dreamwork process are a diary and something to write with. Many people think they can remember their dreams without the need to write them down, but dreams can be very elusive creatures and it is all too easy to find yourself holding on to the bare bones of the imagery while the finer details have trickled away. Some of those details can be vital clues to the meaning of the dream as a whole.

The dream diary also acts over time as a journal, which serves three purposes:

1. A dream that is not immediately understood can be recorded and then left to 'stand' for a while so that the symbols and images can be digested by the dreamer's unconscious. On rereading the dream some time later, it is often found that more connections become obvious and the message of the dream makes more sense. Like all symbolic imagery, dreams have many layers of meaning and some dreams can still be teaching you new things even though they may have been dreamt years ago. In fact, not all dreams are meant to be assimilated immediately as they may contain archetypal (that is, primordial) imagery which underpins the very goal of a person's life.

2. Very often, over time, themes will recur in the dreams and these may not always be apparent until several dreams have been recorded. This is often the psyche's way of trying to get a particular message through to us by using emphasis, especially when we are stuck on some issue in our development. After a while we begin to see the need to tackle the issue that is being shown to us before we can move on.

3. It is always interesting to be able to look back at the way the dream characters and situations develop and evolve. What started out initially as rather primitive attempts to deal with feelings and energies can be seen in later dreams as a coming-to-terms with aspects of the inner self. New, more mature images emerge as the dreamer grows in understanding, and the journal can be a valuable way of mapping one's psychological development.

Basically, then, you will need to set up a positive channel of communication with your dreamlife, and buying your diary or notebook is the first positive step that you will take in programming your mind to retain the dream symbols and messages. Keep your dream diary and a pen by your bed and try to make life easy by having a light source to hand – a bedside lamp, candle or torch. If you have to get up to turn on the light, it is easier to turn over and go back to sleep – and then the dream can be lost for ever!

Some people find the act of writing itself too much of an effort, especially in the early hours of the morning, and prefer to have a tape recorder by the bed into which they can speak as soon as they wake up. However, it is not easy to see patterns in the dream imagery over several days unless you can find time later in the day to transcribe each tape into a diary. Where tape recorders have a short-term advantage is that a tape is usually more immediately decipherable than a note written in a book. If you have ever recorded your dreams in that half-awake state, writing whilst you are still horizontal, you will know that they are not always easy to understand when you come to reread them in the cold light of day. Very often they take on the appearance of a string of hieroglyphics sliding off the page at an angle! Nevertheless, I find that writing down my dreams is more rewarding and more practical, for the reasons given above regarding the benefits of a dream diary.

The second step in the encouragement of your dreamlife is to ask. That is, before you go to sleep at night direct your attention to asking for a dream, perhaps by focusing on a particular issue in your life that you would like to understand more fully, and visualize yourself remembering and recording the dream in the morning. In this way you are influencing your unconscious mind to connect with you as you rise to conscious awareness, and you are more likely to awaken during a period of REM sleep. You will then find that, once you have recorded your first dream and and enjoyed the process of interpreting it, or at least attending to it, the dreams will begin to flow more freely. Perhaps you can regard them as fish lying beneath the surface of the water; if you begin to feed them regularly, they will turn up at feeding time. Similarly, if you want to catch one it can be very elusive, so just catch the 'tail of the fish' – the tail-end of a dream – and you will probably find that the rest of the dream will follow.

Apart from recording the date of the dream and its details, try to recall any events from the preceding day or week that have been on your mind. Very often the dream will make more sense in the light of such events, as our psyche is usually helping us to find solutions to that week's situations, whether they are practical, emotional or connected with health. Without the context, some dreams may be of intellectual interest, but they will be of little use to the dreamer. Also, be very aware of your feelings during and on awakening from the dream, and remember to make a note of them. Feelings and atmospheres are powerful energies that connect you to the deeper layers of your own life process, to past memories and even old traumas, as a way through to healing them.

SUMMARY

- Buy a diary or notebook for recording your dreams. This is your dream diary.

- The diary serves several purposes.
  - It allows you to 'earth' a dream by writing it down, thus encouraging your psyche to give you more.
  - It allows you to incubate a dream and keep working on it.
  - It allows you to recognise recurring themes and images over time.
  - It allows you to review your dreams and see their progress and transformation over time.

- Keep the diary and pen by your bed and near a source of light, or use a tape recorder if you prefer.

- Remember to ask your unconscious for a dream, and before you go to sleep focus on an issue about which you may want some help or guidance.

- When recording the dream on awakening, note down the date and also any events from the previous day or week that may have contributed to the dream.

- Be aware of the feeling content of the dream and any feelings you are left with on awakening.

CHAPTER 6

Where Am I?

IT MAY COME as some surprise to know that everything and every-one in a dream is an aspect of the dreamer, be it a tree, an ink smudge or the next-door neighbour. (This excludes certain dreams such as those called precognitive, which warn of events to come; I shall not be dealing with these here.) If you have not worked with symbolic imagery before, this concept may take some getting used to as those of us in the Western world are generally focused in our conscious minds, which like to take things at face value.

Having said that, dreams can be interpreted on many levels; if there is, say, an interaction in the dream between you (the dreamer) and a person known to you, this will probably reflect a situation happening to you in reality. It will also give you an opportunity to integrate that person's energy into your own by understanding how you project your unconscious processes on to him or her. This way of understanding dreams will become clearer as we go on, using examples as illustration.

Basically then, the dream speaks to us in symbolic language and it is important to try to see the world around us as a reflection of our own values, attitudes and feelings. Your attention will be drawn to certain objects, people and places in the world around you, either because you like them or because you dislike them. Those aspects to which you are indifferent will seldom arise in your dream world, because dreams are a way of teaching us to resolve emotional issues and to gain fresh insight into our motivations and needs. They also give us a chance to view the world in a different way and free ourselves from old attitudes that might hamper our progress. If you find that you have no immediate reaction or association to a particular dream symbol, then it may need a bit more time or some lateral thinking before its relevance in your life is revealed.

The Setting

The first thing to note is the setting of your dream. Is it in a house, a room, a field, a car …? If so, is this setting familiar to you, and how do you feel about the space that you find yourself in? The setting of the dream is like the emotional backdrop that your psyche is using as a basis for the content that is being enacted. It will, therefore, ususally be describing something of the nature or issue that your psyche has chosen to work on. If, for example, you find yourself in a particular room in a house, make a note of what is in the room. How do you feel in the room? Is it dark, dirty, bare, cluttered? Is there something unusual about it?

The house is where we have our sense of belonging, our base. In a dream it often depicts our sense of Self and the quality of our sense of self-worth. Each room in the house can direct us to specific areas of our lives or psyche. The bedroom, for example, can symbolize our sense of resting, peace, sexuality or sensuality. The living room is the place in the house where we mostly 'live'. It often contains the fire or hearth (also the heart/hearth of our nature) and is a place where family and friends gather. The kitchen is a place of nourishment and assimilation, whether of food, ideas or feelings. The toilet is a place where we are instinctual beings, dealing with basic drives and the processes of elimination. The bathroom is for cleansing and healing, and so on.

We may dream of our own house and find we are in a room that we never knew was there. This is our psyche showing us that we have untapped potential or new room for growth; maybe a new experience is entering our life. If we dream of a room or house that is untidy or dirty, this may be how we feel inside – disorganized and neglected. The dream is asking us to attend to ourselves or 'put our house in order'.

It is also important to note the age of the house you are in. A very old house could be your dream directing you to look at your past; perhaps you may have some rather outmoded ideas or old-fashioned morals that colour your life in some way. Even more pertinent, you may dream of living in your old childhood home. This will be your psyche giving you very specific clues from your childhood that are somehow relevant to your present situation or problem.

If your dream is set in the countryside, it represents being in touch with your nature in its most real and elemental aspect. Most people go out into the countryside to feel free, to refresh themselves and to get in touch with their feelings and senses again. The point to note if your dream is set in the countryside is what the weather conditions are like. The weather will depict your moods – your sense of foreboding (dark and glowering) or optimism (bright and warm); your indecision and confusion (fog and mists) or rigidity and emotional constrictions (ice and snow). These are merely suggestions; it is for you to feel your way into the atmosphere that surrounds you in the dream, so that you can gain some sense of the emotional climate that you are dealing with.

Look carefully also at the terrain; are you in desert, jungle, meadowland or mountains? If you are in a desert, for example, are you feeling drained of emotional energy in your life – all dried up and devoid of creative potential? Your psyche may well set your dream in a desert if you are feeling cut off from your feelings or are isolated in some way. But the important thing is to make your *own* associations with the idea of a desert. One of my clients regularly fantasized about being in the desert because of the sheer peace and serenity that it evoked for her personally.

If you are on a mountain top, you may be needing to rise above some situation and get a clearer view. Alternatively, you may simply be feeling on top of the world. Or perhaps you need to conquer or master some skill or to attain a sense of achievement in an area of your life – inner or outer. You might find yourself in swampy, marshy land. Are you 'bogged down' in some situation? We often talk about 'getting that sinking feeling' in the pit of our stomach when we hear bad news or have a sense of failure or disappointment. We are, literally, not on safe ground.

Another setting for the dream may be some form of transport. You may find yourself on a bus or train or in a car, so you need to think about your associations with these vehicles. If, for example, you usually take a train to work, then the train might make you

think about your work routine. Or do you associate trains with pleasure, adventure or meeting relations and friends? It might even be saying something about the speed at which you are living your life at present.

Public transport generally conveys groups of people, and in dreams groups of people or anonymous crowds often signify the unconscious element of a person's psyche. Hence, public transport often indicates that the dreamer is being carried along to some extent by his or her unconscious drives or feelings. On public transport you have no option but to be a passenger – unless, of course, you are a bus or train driver in your waking life. As a passenger you are in a dependent and passive role. This may well be your dream directing you to look at this role or behaviour in your life, so that you can consider acting and thinking in a more independent way in the future.

If you find yourself in a car, are you going fast or slowly? Are you unable to start or stop? This will help you to sense something of the pace of your life or perhaps your inertia. Are you in an old banger, or in a luxurious modern car? If you are driving the car, then you have control of the vehicle (your life's direction); you are not being driven by outside influences. If you are a passenger, look carefully to see who is driving and how you feel about that person in reality. If it is not somebody you know, you need to ask yourself what kind of feelings you have about this person. This will usually indicate some aspect of your own feeling nature that is driving you in life; alternatively, if that person comes as a surprise to you, it may indicate some aspect that you would wish to be predominant or that you are being introduced to as an unconscious driving force in your life.

What if you find yourself riding a bicycle? This is a good sign, meaning that you are in control of your life's direction – you are directly responsible for the energy you put into it. However, travelling on foot in your dreams is *the* most stable form of transport that you can have!

Even within a single dream you may find that you will change between various forms of transport as the dream progresses. Understanding the significance of each form will help you to chart your progress through the dream.

So there are many settings for your dream, depending on what your higher consciousness is trying to tell you. Try to imagine what the following settings would evoke for you: a wood, a church, a barn, a mountain top, an ocean liner, a penny-farthing, a baker's shop, a tent. Each one will have associations that are unique to you, so practise trusting your intuition to guide you.

Aspects of Nature

The same questions need to be asked of each person, animal or object in your dreams: 'What does this mean to me? What does this remind me of or make me feel?' Remember that your dream characters are *personal to you*; it is for this very reason that this book is not attempting to provide a list of symbols or interpretations. I am not absolutely convinced of the concept of universal meanings for symbols as put forward by the authors of some dream dictionaries. If in doubt, attention must be paid to aspects of the dream character that give clues to its significance in the dreamer's life – for instance, the colour, shape, movement, size or 'voice' within the context of its setting. If the dreamer still cannot make sense of the significance, he can always dialogue directly with the dream character using a technique called active imagination, which I shall describe later.

One thing you can be sure of when animals, birds, fish and other creatures enter your dream is that you are dealing with some aspect of your instinctual nature. A lot will depend on your attitude to the creature in question and the feelings it evokes. For example, some people fear snakes or even dread them. For others they evoke fascination and sensuality. Writhing snakes may represent unconscious desires or fears. Because of the snake's resemblance to a penis, the dreamer's attitude to sexuality might need some attention. Is your sexuality giving you cause for concern? Or is your creative energy being blocked and therefore causing you problems of some kind? Repressed and untapped creative energy can lead to frustration and anger. Compare the snake on its belly to the raised cobra swaying to the piper's music; in the latter we see sexual/creative energy that is harnessed and 'in tune' with the person's wishes. While consciousness is raised and focused, it will be no threat or danger to the dreamer.

Birds are creatures of the air and may depict the realm of the spirit, flying free of all earthly concerns. However, your dream bird may be trapped or caged; this may suggest that in some aspect of your life you feel tied down and unable to express your true self or to live out your aspirations. You might dream of geese, for example, and they may appear in your dream simply to remind you of your childhood holidays on a farm and associated feelings of innocence and long summer days. With all creatures you will usually be led to some instinctual feeling that needs integrating into your reality.

Throughout the ages animals and birds have been associated with certain qualities and characteristics – stubborn as a mule, timid as a mouse, strong as an ox, mad as a March hare and so on. We may think of dogs as loyal, cats as independent, cuckoos as greedy, lions as regal and badgers as secretive. However, if you happen to have found a stray cat when you were seven years old and brought it home only to be told that you could not keep it, the memories that a cat triggers for you may be more to do with pain and loss than with independence. Again, we have to think with the holistic and subjective right brain and not be too fixed in our associations with these images.

Take note of what is happening to the creatures in your dream. Are they chasing you, or are you chasing them? Are they trapped, playing, aggressive, frightened or loving? Look at their size, too; are they out of proportion in some way? If you have an elephant the size of a mouse or a mouse the size of an elephant, something within your instinctual nature needs rebalancing. The permutations and combinations of animal or creature symbols can be a very rich expression of your own feeling or instinctual nature.

The psyche, too, can be very inventive in its attempts to enlighten us, and the creatures in our dreams may be mythical or magical. Some will be composites of several creatures and, depending on their composition, will represent the growth and alchemy of our inner development. Other creatures may transform themselves with ease. A fish might suddenly turn into a rabbit and show us how our unconscious urges (fish/water) are being transformed and made more tangible (rabbit/earth). A cow, a creature of the earth, may suddenly sprout wings and take to the sky. This may suggest that some element of our instinctual nature is being raised to the element of the rational mind (air) – or perhaps we are indulging in a flight of fancy! We may even be wanting to rise above the mundane aspects of our everyday existence. When I explore the significance of the elements, in Chapter 7, such transformations will be easier to understand.

Flowers too can reflect our feelings. We often pick or buy flowers to thank people or to enhance the beauty and atmosphere of our own homes. Shakespeare used the language of flowers, as have many writers and poets throughout the ages. Again, it is what the flower means to *you* that matters. To one person a lily may be associated with morbidity and funerals, while to another person it may be a prized possession and symbolic of purity and innocence. Note the colour of the flower that your psyche picks, because in any context, colours are highly evocative.

Colours play a big part in imagery, and many people have a vivid recall of colour in their dreams. Our dreams often give us guidance about the use of colour in our lives, either as an aid to healing or simply to inject a new vitality into our feeling spectrum. Even if you are not a colour-conscious person you will probably make several subjective connections with the colour red, for example. If you find yourself wearing a red dress or a red tie in a dream and you would not normally think of wearing this colour, ask yourself why you avoid it. Does it make you feel self-conscious? Do you think it is 'cheap'? Or would you secretly like to wear red because it is rather daring? This may be saying something about your ability to express whatever red means to you. After all, some part of you obviously chose to do so in your dream when your usual inhibitions were not in control!

Again, you only have to reflect on the way we use colour in our everyday speech to see how much it influences us, if only unconsciously: seeing red, feeling blue, green with envy, black moods, yellow-bellied, in the pink and so on. We all have favourite colours; some of us actively avoid certain colours. There are usually reasons, even if it is 'because my Grandma said green was unlucky'. Whatever the colour, try to make your own associations with it.

So colour, form, symbolism, association, activity, element and transformation are all coordinates to be held in the balance as you search for the significance of each creature, plant or object in your dreamlife. Try not to overlook any aspect of your dream or dismiss it as irrelevant, because the psyche is very particular in its choice of material for the 'props' and scenery of these amazing dramas.

SUMMARY

- Everything and everyone in your dream is an aspect of *you*.

- The setting of the dream provides the background to the issue that your psyche has chosen to work on.

- Houses and homes depict your sense of Self; the rooms represent the different aspects of the psyche. The age of a house or building may give clues to the past or to past patterns of behaviour.

- A countryside setting represents your own basic disposition, and the conditions of the weather and terrain will indicate your moods and state of mind.

- Vehicles show you how you are travelling along your path in life at any given time. Are you in control or being driven? Do you know where you are going, and how are you using your energy or drive?

- Animals or creatures represent aspects of your instinctual nature. What association do you have with them?

- Size of creatures, the manner in which they act and their relationship to you all say something about the expression of your own feelings or instinctive reactions. These feelings are capable of transforming and developing within the dream.

- Flowers, too, depict our feelings and the blossoming (or withering) of some aspect of our nature.

- Colours describe moods and emotions, but they can also be prescribing certain healing energies.

- Always listen to your own personal associations concerning colour, form and symbolism. The dream imagery is unique to you.

CHAPTER 7

The Elements

SINCE THE BEGINNING of time the elements of fire, earth, air and water have been with us and part of us. They have been used to understand and describe our nature and emotional energy since man took an interest in his own psyche. During the Renaissance, philosophers described people as belonging to one of four temperaments based on the theory of 'humours' or fluids of the body: the Sanguine (airy), Choleric (fiery), Phlegmatic (watery) and Melancholic (earthy).

The elements have been incorporated into our language, and they are most noticeable when we attempt to describe ourselves and others. We may use phrases like 'fiery temperament', 'airy-fairy', 'a bit wet' or 'an earthy character'. Jung associated each element with a particular function of human nature. Fire represents the intuitive function, air is the intellect, earth is the sensation function and water is symbolic of the feeling realm.

Fiery types have the ability to perceive the undercurrents in a situation and often have a 'hunch' about the present or the future. Because they are spontaneous people, they are not ones to dwell on the past very much but like to test and develop their creative potential 'now'. Creatures of vision and power, they can also find that their 'power' builds up into volatile energy at times, emerging as strong physical desires, anger or 'bloody-mindedness' if not given freedom of expression.

Although at home with their energy and drive, they are not always so good at earthing their visions; they need to recognize that their intuition must be practically realized for it to be of any benefit.

Water types are like the ever-changing ebb and flow of the oceans, swimming in the energies of compassion and empathy. Water types often respond and react based on unconscious evaluations of people and situations. They are nurturing or motherly types, both men and women. In the French language the root of the word for 'Mother', *mère*, is the same as that for 'sea', *mer*. It is also interesting that our word 'mother' can be found in the word 'smother', as there can be the tendency for water types to overwhelm others with their concern. Water people are very sensitive to atmospheres and have an instinctive understanding of the needs of others, but it would be useful for them to learn when and how to rationalize their feelings and thus make them more conscious.

Earth types are generally sensual, realistic and practical. They understand life by building a body of knowledge and experience based on facts and 'common sense'. They enjoy the ability to satisfy their physical desires and appetites and are able to handle their finances and responsibilities with relative ease. They are, when positive, more comfortable than other types with their own bodies and with 'making a living', but this can also be their downfall. Over-identification with physical materiality can blinker them to other forms of experience, such as intuition, spirituality or imagination, that may not depend on facts. They need to see that security can also come from inner 'knowing' and not simply from material accumulation.

Air types are also rational people but they have a need to be free-flowing and unrestrained in their experiences like the wind, blowing where it wills. They like to play with ideas and are good at communicating. We use the expression 'air-waves' when talking about radio and television, which are both media of communication. Air types use their thinking function to categorize and understand the world, but often to the exclusion of reference to their feelings. Although safe with the realm of ideas, they are not always able to feel safe without such a framework of logic. But some aspects of life, such as the feeling nature, *are* illogical and irrational, which demands relinquishing the controls of the mind. Air types sometimes need to learn how to dive into the water from their high-dive boards, otherwise they can be trapped in the ivory towers of their intellect and feel very alone.

We each tend to conform predominantly to one of these types in our psychological behaviour. However, when it comes to the smaller cycles of day-to-day behaviour we may display aspects of each element at various times. We may also for a time get stuck in a particular mode of behaviour to the exclusion of all others; when this happens, our psyche will attempt to redress the balance at night through the symbolism of our dreams.

Fire

The element of fire may manifest in a dream in numerous ways. We may find ourselves literally playing with fire or with a burning object, which might indicate anything from our desire to take risks to getting ourselves involved in some situation which is 'too hot to handle'. If the fire is out of control, we may need to rein in our desires over something; alternatively, it may be that we are simply afraid of our desires or sexuality, and further work on the dream will show us that there is nothing to worry about as we learn how to deal with the fire.

We might also find that we want to seek out a source of heat because we are too cold in our dream. This would mirror the fact that we are not really in touch with our vital energy and are feeling 'out in the cold' on some issue.

Fire being a creative energy, it is important to know how to respect it and channel it in the most positive way we can. It is also, at a higher level, symbolic of our spiritual energy and our 'will to be', which can manifest in dreams as both heat and light. The sun, therefore, would be a potent symbol for our very essence. If it shines in our dreams, that might indicate that the emotional/spiritual climate of our life is going well. But if we are in a desert and thirsty, we may need to attenuate our will, ambition or spiritual fervour by listening also to our feelings (water) – otherwise we are in danger of getting 'all burnt out'.

Fire shows us how to be assertive, courageous and passionate. We talk of 'burning desires' and 'heated debate'. If we are afraid, we get 'cold feet' and if anxious or annoyed we get 'hot under the collar'. And finally, recognize the flames of anger which also might be out of control. If the fire in your dreams is destructive and all-consuming, ask yourself if your blood is 'boiling' about someone or something. Maybe you are angry with yourself for some reason and are not expressing it openly but turning the anger destructively into yourself. There are no good or bad judgements involved here. Your dream is simply describing a certain energy and helping you to understand and balance it.

Water

Something about water, the element of feeling, can be understood from the way we use it in language. We can 'flow with our feelings' or 'gush with sentiment'; we 'bubble with laughter' and 'feel all at sea'; we can have 'waves of sadness', feel 'all churned up' or have that 'sinking feeling'. Because water is a great reflector, it also has a connection with our imagination, the unconscious and our psychic ability. We may dream of diving into the ocean and bringing up a pearl or some object of great meaning to us. The psyche might be telling us to plumb our own hidden depths and look below the surface of our conscious minds for answers. Just as frantic currents may rage on the surface of rivers or seas and yet the water beneath is calm, so too must we learn to dive beneath the surface of life and still our emotions at times, if only for peace and rest.

In the same way that the analogy of the desert was used above, we can also dam up our feelings and may dream of such a dam; this could indicate that we need to learn to release a blocked water-source/feeling, perhaps a little at a time, through active imagination. We might dream about drowning and gasping for air, which would teach us that we need to bring some rationality to our feelings or some space into a demanding situation. Frozen water, of course, manifests as ice and some part of us may feel cold, frigid or cut off emotionally. We must ask ourselves how we can warm it up.

Remembering the link with *la mer* and mother, the sea has associations with the womb and birth. Being on the sea or in it in a dream may symbolize that we are as yet in an undifferentiated state at the feeling level, perhaps still identifying too closely with our mother's psyche and needs or living too much in a fantasy world.

Conversely (and this is where it is useful to know where we are in our inner development), this dream could be showing us that we have come full circle and can dispense with our ego needs at last – we can merge our consciousness with that greater ocean of life, thus experiencing a kind of spiritual rebirth.

Water is also a great cleanser and purifier. Christ was baptised in water and it is often used as a consecratory symbol. If you find yourself bathing or washing yourself in a dream, you may be needing to heal or purify some aspect of your nature or 'wash your hands' of some affair. It may indicate that you feel some aspect of your feeling nature to be impure or, if you are washing your whole body or your clothes, that you wish to make a 'clean break' or a fresh start into a new cycle of your life.

Earth

There are many images of the earth element that may appear in dreams and, as with water, you must allow your mind to play and associate freely with the various pictures created. Human beings tend not to be very good at living 'in the now' and being in touch with their instinctual nature; we are usually either thinking ahead of ourselves or dwelling on the past. We can so easily lose contact with our own natural rhythms, and because of this we often find that our bodies have to complain loudly to us by being ill or stressed. If we are listening to our psyche, however, we will often get clues about the presence of an imbalance long before any illness reveals itself.

As mentioned earlier, the kind of ground we are walking or travelling on in our dreams is very important. Are you on solid ground, or on shifting sands and unable to move forward easily? The ground beneath us has a lot to do with our feelings of security. If it feels as though the ground is always giving way under us we may need to work on supporting our inner needs more firmly and 'standing our ground' when challenged. Or we might feel that we are under the earth, in a cave or tunnel. Do we need to unearth certain memories or experiences from our unconscious and 'dig deeper'?

Creatures of the earth may also figure predominantly to remind us of our instinctual nature. It is surprising how many moles appear in the dreams of clients when first entering therapy! Most animals signify a need to get back to basics in our lives.

Dreams of vegetables, plants and flowers are also telling us to focus on our vegetative and instinctual functions – but take heed, for some plants or vegetables may appear in our dreams because our psyche knows that our body needs certain foodstuffs or vitamins at a particular time. If, after dreaming of spinach, we find during the course of a day that a market-seller is trying to sell us two bunches of spinach for the price of one, we would do well to take up the offer!

And then there are dreams where our bodies or parts of them are in pain, under attack, severed or maybe being decorated or attended to in some loving way. Be aware of the particular region of your body that is the focus of such attention. This aspect of body awareness will be dealt with more fully in Chapter 13.

Air

In our dreams we may find ourselves floating or flying in the air, and we then need to ask the following questions:

(1) Are we enjoying the experience and the freedom that this gives us, or

(2) Do we want to come down to the ground but cannot?

Sometimes we can get too 'bogged down' with the trivia of life, or too immersed in a particular feeling or rut. Our psyche is trying to compensate by showing us that we can rise above these matters and see things from a different perspective. Leaving behind the constraints of limited thinking, we are allowing ourselves to feel that our self-made prison is an illusion and that we truly *can* free ourselves and move into different dimensions and spaces. Techniques such as meditation, relaxation, creativity and active imagination can all be used to move beyond our normal and somewhat limited state of awareness.

At other times we may be getting too lost in our rational mind, or maybe we are avoiding dealing with certain basic and pressing issues by escaping into the element of air and becoming 'airy-fairy'.

Perhaps we are avoiding a commitment, procrastina[ting], [wanting] to be somewhere else. In this case we really need to ['come down to earth']. We need our feet on the ground, and we can [use our imag]ination to bring ourselves back and to feel what it is [in the] situation that we are trying to leave. What kind of help would we need in order to feel safe and strong enough to tackle our particular life situation? (Active imagination will be dealt with in Chapter 8.)

When air is in motion, of course, it may manifest as wind or even as a hurricane. This could indicate a need for the winds of change to blow through a problem – perhaps we are causing ourselves unnecessary stress by 'brain-storming'. We may feel buffeted around by the ideas and attitudes of others, and need to know how to stand firm and resist.

Air in our dreams can also symbolize the breath of life or the realm of the Spirit, or vital energy, which animates us. If we are suffocating or being suffocated, we must observe who is doing this to us. Are we restricting ourselves from fully entering into life and achieving our potential? Are we allowing others to do this to us? Or do we feel that our freedom is being eroded somewhere?

And finally, the elements may also work together in our dreams; for instance, a tornado may start on the land and end in the water; mud is a mixture of earth and water; condensation is moisture that can form in the air; wind can blow flames; fire can cause water to dry up or earth to scorch. When the elements occur in twos or threes it may be a question of seeing how one aspect of your nature affects another, or you might need to achieve a balance of functions in your life.

Jung described dreams as an alchemical process in which psychic energy is continually changing and transforming to produce new growth and development. As you get more practised at reading your own moods and cycles it will become easier to relate your dreams to the process that is trying to evolve within you. As you learn to trust your dreams you will also allow them to guide you to make the necessary changes and adjustments in your external reality conducive to your own inner well-being.

SUMMARY

- The elements are often used in language to describe character and temperament. Jung associated each element with a particular function of human nature.

- Fire types are intuitive and spontaneous; water types are emotional and sensitive; earth types are realistic and practical; and air types are rational and good at communicating.

- We may be predominantly one psychological type, but at various times we display aspects of each element. Sometimes we need to adjust the balance.

- Fire and heat themes (or the lack of them) in our dreams will show us how we are dealing with our desires, will, creativity and sexuality.

- Water themes (or the lack of them) constitute not only an element of the feeling nature but also illustrate our imagination and connection to the unconscious. Water has associations with the womb and the source of all being. It is also a cleanser and purifier.

- Earth themes (or the lack of them) are associated with our physical and instinctual nature. Earth is connected with our sense of security and sustenance.

- Air themes (or the lack of them) show us how we are using our intellect and rationality. Air can represent the flow of thoughts and a sense of freedom. It also depicts the spirit.

- Elements may change and affect each other within a dream, thus describing the transformation of psychic energy within us.

CHAPTER 8

Interaction Techniques 1

Active Imagination or Guided Imagery

IT MIGHT BE useful at this point to introduce some techniques that will help you take a more dynamic approach to working with your dreams. Later on we shall be looking in greater depth at the people who enter your dreams and issues such as the masculine and feminine principles that they represent, as well as the function of what is known as the Shadow. I mentioned active imagination earlier; along with the technique of Gestalt, which I shall describe in more detail in Chapter 9, I have found it an invaluable tool for understanding dreams and developing them more fully.

So far I have been posing a lot of questions that need to be asked about the various symbols, situations and characters that appear in dreams. Many will have immediate associations that can be made consciously and with a certainty that will unfold the deeper meaning and feelings behind the symbol. However, some will remain a mystery and it will be difficult to understand their significance or relevance to the dreamer's life. In such cases, one can put the dream to one side for a while and allow the unconscious mind to work on it over time. Very often the significance becomes clearer and associations will suddenly come 'out of the blue'. The subtlety of the symbols will be intuited, rather as a name or tune will come to mind several hours or even days after you have been struggling to recall it.

Because symbols are born of the unconscious mind, they do not readily offer up their meaning to conscious rationalizing. Rather, we need to meet them on home ground and allow the mind to play in a relaxed way, giving the symbol a chance to impress itself into our awareness at a deeper level. After all, the psyche has carefully coded its contents for a reason – otherwise we would dream about issues in a much more literal way. One of the functions of dreams is to release potential at a feeling and creative level, and our rational mind is not always ready to accept that which the unconscious mind reveals in its full reality. Sometimes we are being reminded of, and reconnected to, feelings and memories which have been 'shelved' for many years, and there is a resistance to the process either because the feelings are initially painful or simply because we do not feel prepared to move on, even when the feelings are good. All growth involves change, and the dreamer must be prepared to meet the challenge of the growth process if he or she wants to embark on this journey.

The other way of meeting the symbol on its own level is to go back into the dream and ask the relevant questions. This does not entail going back to sleep on purpose (however tempting!) but simply relaxing the body, closing one's eyes, slowing the breathing slightly and allowing oneself to recall the dream as vividly as it was experienced initially. This time, however, you actively explore the dream scenario and enter into a dialogue with the dream characters. This technique is called guided imagery or active imagination, and was introduced by Carl Jung. Active imagination enables the dreamer to elicit information by becoming an active participant in the dream process rather than remaining a passive observer/recorder. Whilst dreaming, it feels as though we are organically part of the flow of sensations and feelings; but this experience soon fades as we surface to our waking state. But we can get back in there if we want, and change certain reactions or approaches that did not feel good at the time. A client of mine called Pam, a woman in her mid-thirties, had the following dream:

Pam and her husband Dave drive to a warehouse where there is a lot of junk and old clothes. They get out of the car. Pam's twin sister Jenny is there. Pam feels that her husband is very interested in Jenny because they talk a lot together and Dave ignores Pam, who then feels excluded. They all get into the car – a new car – and Dave says to Jenny, 'Why don't you get into the driver's seat and I'll show you how the gears work'. Pam, feeling miserable and a failure, gets into the back seat while Dave demonstrates the car to Jenny. But eventually Pam gets angry and shouts, 'Damn you, why are you ignoring me?' She just keeps repeating these words, getting more and more upset, but there is no reaction from the other two. It is as though she is not there. She decides to get out of the car, and stands on the pavement feeling unloved.

The first stage of dealing with a dream is, of course, to make the associations. As she and I explored each element together, we saw that Pam's twin sister (Jenny) represents a lot of the qualities within Pam that were repressed and unconscious, the Shadow side of Pam's nature. (We will deal with the shadow in Chapter 11.)

Pam described her sister as bright, bubbly, outgoing and attractive, but she talked of herself as withdrawn, introverted and fearful. Pam's fears at the time of the dream were that her husband was losing interest in her, and she was aware of feeling cut off and distant. The more she suppressed her feminine sensuality and assertiveness, the more she feared her husband would leave her. All suppressed instinctual energy becomes larger than life to the dreamer. In this case the 'bubbly' part of Pam appeared to take over both the driver's seat (control) and her husband's attention whilst Pam was pushed into the back seat or the unconscious. Also pushed into the back seat was her anger at being ignored, which reflected her denial of her own self-worth. In reality Pam admitted that she had never felt able to express her anger openly: the dream told her how much anger was within her but also that she was unable to communicate it to anyone. The result was frustration.

The setting of the dream is a warehouse full of junk, which suggests that the dreamer is going to be dealing with some issue of neglect or abandonment. As Pam and I talked through her dream she recalled how, being one of four children in her family, she had always felt ignored and her needs unrespected. She felt particularly angry with her father, and the dream reminded her of the time when she was five years old, helpless and powerless. She had desperately wanted guidance and support from him, but her needs were not met or responded to and so she had had to bury her rage – 'I had to freeze the caring and loving part'. At fourteen, when she again needed some guidance and direction, it was not there. Her parents were often away at weekends. In particular, Pam told me, 'Whenever I made or underwent any changes in my life they were not talked about or shared'. In the dream Pam watches Dave supporting and guiding Jenny through the 'gear changes' and gets increasingly more outraged at witnessing what she never had. Adolescence (the gear changes) was a time when her sexuality was emerging, and these changes also went unacknowledged.

We decided, therefore, to go back into the dream using active imagination. Pam would then contact the feeling content of the dream with conscious awareness, and decide how she needed to react in order to change this particular complex. First of all she made herself comfortable in her chair.

If the dreamer feels particularly tense it is often useful to go through a relaxation exercise, because tension can distract from the concentration necessary to stay with the imagery. External sounds must be kept to the minimum too. Guided imagery is a meditative state, and it can be very distressing to be jolted out of this level of awareness by a sudden noise. Some people may wish to lie down for the exercise, but others find the horizontal position makes them feel too vulnerable, especially if the dream content is in any way threatening. In this position there is also a greater possibility of actually falling asleep.

Imagery can be easily monitored by the dreamer without outside guidance, although it may be helpful initially to have somebody present as a guide. The guide can:

(1) help to direct the dreamer back into the dream scene

(2) elicit information about the feeling content, and

(3) take relevant notes about any changes that the dreamer undertakes or experiences. This last point can be of particular use for future reference. As in actual dreaming, when one leaves the imagery state there can be a certain amount of detail lost 'in transit'.

However, the guide must not intrude on the dreamer's imaging process. The guide is there merely to help the dreamer to focus attention and to act as a recorder of events; therefore any communication needs to be done in quiet tones. It is helpful also for the guide to sit near enough to the dreamer so that the dreamer's voice can be heard. If the dreamer goes deeply into the relaxed state, the voice often becomes quiet and may even be slightly slurred. It will not help him or her to concentrate if the guide is consistently asking for sentences to be repeated!

Pam relaxed in the chair and I talked her back into the dream. She found herself in the back seat of the car again. This time, however, I asked her if she would like to change the way that she dealt with the situation. Pam decided to get out of the back seat and confront Dave with her anger face-to-face instead of railing at him from behind. She observed that Dave was very taken aback by this open confrontation, and that she was feeling very excited as she expressed her power by looking him straight in the eyes. She asked him why he was ignoring her and paying so much attention to Jenny. This time the dream character of Dave answered that it was because Pam was so introverted and he could not reach her. At least he was getting some response from Jenny who was giving him love, showing an interest in him and seeing him as a complete person. He said that Pam did not attend to his needs for love and respect. Pam acknowledged what he said and then decided to take over the controls of the car and drive everyone home. This time, however, she chose to get into her own car, not the dream car, and the experience was quite different. She felt in touch with her own power and she did not let her fears overwhelm her. She became aware of leaning back into the driver's seat and feeling very comfortable. I then talked Pam back to the fully wakened state.

In talking over the experience afterwards, Pam acknowledged that she never really openly declared her needs – or her anger – to her husband. Blocking her anger was also blocking her creative energy, however, and she knew that Dave would respect her far more if she could learn to express herself more openly. She also acknowledged that she did not respect Dave's vulnerable side or give enough attention to his sensitivity or needs.

Basically this was because she had also blocked off her own sensitivity, as a defence. She talked to me about having lost her poetic vision, creativity and drive and how she would love to be involved in poetry, acting and lecturing. From this experience of active imagination she had learnt that it was possible to empower herself by making changes on the inner levels of awareness (in other words, becoming the 'Jenny' part of her), which then manifested outwardly as creative solutions.

With these kinds of insights it can be seen how the dream strives to demonstrate healing properties by showing the dreamer the elements in life that are out of balance and in need of some fine-tuning and awareness. It is fun to work on your dreams in this way but it is very important to practise the art of 'letting go' – that is, allowing the dream characters to offer their advice spontaneously without trying to control the outcome. It can be very tempting to direct the answers yourself. Active imagination demands a certain trust in your own intuitive wisdom as revealed through the dream process. There is a delicate balance to be struck between deciding what you want to change and yet also being open to guidance from the dream characters should some of your choices be inappropriate.

Using this method, you will find that the answers are fresh and new. Many will be sheer revelations! And remember, everything in your dreams can talk to you or show you its significance, whether it be a tree or a dustbin; all you have to do is ask.

SUMMARY

- Active imagination is a process used to re-enter a dream and interact or dialogue with the characters and images.

- Feelings and sensations can be re-created and integrated more fully.

- It is useful to make associations with the dream images initially, but active imagination can also be used on a dream before analysis. If the meaning of the dream is not clear, active imagination may elicit the meaning more immediately.

- Find a quiet room and relax in a chair. Make sure there will be no interruptions.

- Active imagination can be practised alone, but it may be useful at first to have somebody else helping you to direct your focus and to record events. The 'guide' must not be intrusive.

- Aim to elicit information from the key characters in your dream and to try out an alternative course of action, for instance to follow through unfinished business or to confront or react to situations with a more positive or creative approach.

- Practise the art of 'letting go' – allowing the dream characters to offer insights spontaneously without trying to control the outcome. Learn to listen to your inner wisdom and trust the dream process to unfold in a new way.

- Record the results of your active imagination when you have finished, or ask your 'guide' to do this for you while you are in the dream process.

CHAPTER 9

Interaction Techniques 2

Gestalt Chair Work

A FURTHER EXTENSION of active imagination is a process called Gestalt. This is a German term meaning 'form' or 'shape', and Gestalt therapy was originated by the psychotherapist Dr Fritz Perls. He developed the 'empty chair' process, by which fragments of the dream material are isolated and then communicated with by giving them a separate space in the room, such as an empty chair.

Gestalt is based on the idea that the whole is greater than the sum of its parts. Certainly, when dream symbols, characters or objects are contacted individually and then dialogued with in this way, a whole process of transformation and illumination can evolve. Chapter 8 described how the dreamer can contact the dream material through active imagination, but there are times when the character or symbol being questioned does not respond or is in some way elusive and difficult to focus clearly. In such instances I would suggest using Gestalt. This method allows a more dynamic aspect to come into play, a more direct experience in the 'here and now' of both questioning the dream character, symbol or motif and of *becoming* it. Seeing the dream action from the perspective of the various dream elements can give a very immediate sense of understanding and, as a result, an opportunity to resolve apparent conflict situations.

Here is an example of using Gestalt to clarify the meaning of a dream. A client called Colin had the following dream:

'I was with a group of three motorcyclists going around a track. We were dressed in mechanics' overalls. Another group of three dressed in black leather came hurtling up behind us, so we spread out across the track to prevent them from getting past us. They were faster but we stopped them from getting past. I felt we were right to do this because they were louts.'

Colin is an artistic man who was working in therapy on becoming a 'practical artist' – that is, making a living out of his work. He was therefore dealing with issues of self-worth and developing the space to allow his trusting and more vulnerable feelings to be expressed more freely. He was quite controlled in his feeling nature, but had the ability to access his intuitive guidance through dreams and free artistic expression. Often, however, he was aware of blocking his creative spontaneity.

Using the Gestalt method, we decided to give each group of cyclists a label. The group in black leather Colin called 'Speed', and the others he called 'Laid-back'. We set out two chairs, one behind the other, to represent these two groups and I asked Colin whom he would like to get in touch with first. He decided to 'become' Laid-back, and this is what he experienced by sitting on that chair.

'An open track is in front of us and the other two are on my right – I'm on the inside lane. It's a speedway track. There's a loud noise and it makes me wince. I can feel them [the Speed gang] wanting to go straight past so the three of us want to fill up the track. We want to get them to go at our pace. We were here first and we envy their ability to disappear into the distance. We can't let them – it will change us and we won't be in a relaxed state of enjoying the track any more. I'd like them to join us or drop behind. They're impatient. They're aggressive, pushy and nagging and it makes me feel stubborn. I put the brakes on even more and want to block their ability to do better than me.'

Colin then decided to experience the Speed chair.

'We're competitive. We're not having a race and yet we are, and we are joy, exhiliration and speed working smoothly in conjunction as a group. There's a sense of harmony. I feel irritated by them [the Laid-backs] but as if by a fly – it's not serious. We'll leave these people behind. We don't want to cause accidents; we're not louts. They're just older and they envy the coordination of youth. We're

younger, in our mid-twenties, and they're thirty to fifty and piggish. We'll look for a gap. They wear overalls and helmets and they're old-fashioned. We wear black leather and may look threatening. I want to tell them that what they're doing is unnecessary [blocking us]. Are they really enjoying the situation of biking? If so, they shouldn't need to do this. Why don't they let us continue? We could join them but we want to go further, and we find this a funny situation. They're not prepared to listen to us and they've already judged us, but perhaps it would be nicer if they could get together with us for a drink afterwards.'

Here we can see two aspects of Colin's nature in conflict; one is youthful and spontaneous, while the other is older, anxious and inhibiting. The spontaneous energy is seeking integration, but the more habitual aspects of Colin's nature resist this initial attempt to open up to the new awareness. (Notice how Colin goes from a collective 'we' to a more subjective 'I' as he identifies with the energy behind the Laid-backs). But then an interesting change came about as Colin moved into the Laid-back chair again and the more vulnerable side of the character opened up.

'I want to throw out a rope and let them pull me. I'm envious of their ease and harmony. I feel a sense of loss [Colin was feeling tearful at this point]. I've blocked off my youth!' And then – 'It will be OK to let them "be" as long as we can meet them in the pub afterwards. I wouldn't want them to leave us behind.'

Colin then realized that Laid-back had a lot to offer the Speed character. 'It has maturity and experience and the ability to enjoy itself in a relaxed way. It could wave Speed down and take off its [Laid-back's] helmet, and in that way it would be taking off its aggression.'

This was a wonderfully symbolic gesture of breaking down some of Colin's defences against his more spontaneous nature – the helmet represented his fixed attitudes and beliefs about himself, plus the restrictions he had placed on his outlook on life. At this point he was able to turn round in the Laid-back chair and face Speed for the first time: 'That's odd, to see a younger version of myself. It feels threatening, but now we can acknowledge each other. [To Speed] I'd like to ride on your bike.'

In turning around to face what up to this point had been behind him (an unconscious aspect of his own masculinity) Colin felt able to acknowledge the energy, spontaneity and exuberance of his own creative potential, which up till now he had kept in check by certain mental and emotional constructs and defences. Although this was reminiscent of the spontaneity he had once felt in his twenties, he had turned his back on it because at that time, during the 1960s, much of his spontaneity had been released artificially through the use of drugs; he had considered this to be a negative and destructive phase of his life. Even as a young boy of six or seven Colin had felt inhibited from exploring his own initiative and creativity because he had felt himself to be very much under the control and direction of his two older brothers. Consequently he had continued to use these controls on himself in later life, and he was very moved to find that it was possible to begin making a new relationship with this youthful energy.

In taking off the helmet of his defences, Laid-back also revealed the child within the adult whose development had been arrested but whose curiosity and desire to learn were still very much alive. Sometimes we need to go back to areas of our life that were not fully completed earlier, perhaps through lack of opportunity, and pick up the threads again. In this instance, Colin was working with three cycles of his life – childhood, youth and middle age. As the crystallized aspects of Laid-back were melting, the child emerged. Now Speed became the teacher and dispenser of knowledge and new experience.

Sitting in the Speed chair he said, sounding surprised: 'I see him [Laid-back] as a little boy now, not an old man. He was just taking on the gestures of an old person in order to feel safe. I feel sorry for him; he's about six or seven and he wants to ride on the front of the machine.' At this point Colin glimpsed another part of the dream, previously forgotten, where he had sat on Speed's lap and they raced off together. This also illustrates the fact that Gestalt, because it puts one so immediately in touch with the dream energy, can bring back forgotten sensations and missing links in dreams. 'I feel pleased to be able to show him something that I love. He's trusting me, and he'd like to learn to be instinctive too.'

Finally, Colin finished up on the Laid-back/child's chair: 'This is is great! I think I've come closer to what I wanted but didn't know how to ask for it. I thought Speed was unapproachable but he *has* feelings. He's very instinctive, but he needs wisdom. He's maybe a little crazy, too, but I feel safe when he's with me. We need to stay together. He's giving me a sense of fun and I show him vulnerability, but he needs to act with more awareness of others. Now I can feel myself growing up anew and merging with the driver so that I can take control of the machine.'

It is quite useful in this exercise to have an extra chair which can be labelled the Witness or Assessment chair. At various intervals during the Gestalt chair work the subject can sit here to view the process objectively and comment on what is happening to him or her. At the end of the exercise the dreamer can then witness the whole event, assimilate the various characters and meditate on or discuss how these energies can be integrated and expressed in everyday life.

When Colin sat on this Witness chair to assess the whole event he could see that in this exchange of energies he was pulling together the mind and the heart – the academic and the instinctive aspects of his nature, which in their former state had prevented him from feeling safe in trusting his creative power, here symbolized by the motor-bike. While he had blocked his creative energy it had been forced into the unconscious, where it had built up into an aggressive and urgent state. Because the dream focused on the masculine principle, Colin was also trying to get back in touch with his masculinity and learn how to deal with issues like assertiveness and ambition. If he had not made this dream conscious, this inner drive would have continued to make him restless, self-critical and frustrated. Working with Gestalt enabled Colin to move these energies on to a successful development, and it gave him the necessary drive and direction to seek help in setting himself up in business in a more practical and professional manner.

With his new-found sense of empowerment he was able to approach a local business centre that he once would have shunned, and he came to realize that this did not detract from his artistic nature as he had initially feared; rather, it supported him in furthering his business and his self-respect. Taking part in the process of the dream in this direct way enables the dreamer to take a more active part in his life also, thus gaining a new perspective on a situation – which is, after all, what creativity is all about!

SUMMARY

- Gestalt is a German term meaning 'form' or 'shape'. A part or parts of your dream process can be isolated and then communicated with, using the 'empty chair' technique.

- It is a dynamic way to focus on particular characters or symbols, to elicit information and also to experience becoming that character or symbol.

- Choose a dream and decide which characters or symbols you want to isolate. Allocate them spaces or chairs within the room and give them names.

- Do not choose too many characters. Keep things simple and start with two or three until you get used to the process.

- Set out an extra chair for you to sit in as a Witness or Observer. Use this space from time to time as a place from which to assess the progress of the interaction and also to record the events so far.

- As you dialogue with the characters and then become them, solutions and resolutions will emerge as the energy of the characters evolves and transforms.

- Feelings can be confronted, new approaches and insights may emerge, and a healing process and a sense of clarification will usually be effected.

CHAPTER 10

Dream People

AND NOW FOR the people whom we encounter in our dreams. There are two kinds of people in dreams – those you know and those you do not know. With the former you need to work out the quality or basis of your relationship to them in reality – that is, are they on equal terms with you, or dependent on you, or in authority over you in some way? Just as your psyche chooses objects, creatures, colours and so on in order to focus on various inner qualities for your development, so also does it choose people with certain characteristics and for whom you have certain feelings in order to highlight those feelings and attitudes within yourself. Learning from people whom you know will be dealt with in the first part of this chapter. There will also be characters whom you do not know and who will be introducing new energies for you to explore. These we shall deal with later in the chapter.

Both men and women will figure in your dreams as you seek to balance the two sides of your nature, the masculine and the feminine. After many thousands of hours attending to the developmental journeys of his clients in analysis and listening to their many and varied dreams, Jung grew to understand that men personified the feminine psychological tendencies of their psyches, such as feelings, moods, hunches and sensitivity for nature, by female figures in their dreams. He also learned that women personified the masculine psychological tendencies of their psyches – goal-directedness, rational and logical thought, will, aspirations and so on – by male figures. The former he called the 'anima' and the latter the 'animus'.

However, women also need to relate to and develop their feminine nature; likewise, men their masculine nature. So for the purposes of this book it is easier to work on the understanding that, if you dream of a man, you are trying to integrate some aspect of that masculine energy in order to further your development. If there is a woman in your dream she will represent aspects of your feminine nature which need attention, irrespective of whether you, the dreamer, are male or female.

Recognizing the ways in which we are teaching ourselves to increase our self-knowledge through the use of other people in our dreams requires a certain amount of experience in working with different dream scenarios. It is a fairly complex issue because of the variety of ways that the psyche uses to bring us face-to-face with the over-developed and under-developed aspects of our nature. But by listening to what the characters in our dreams say and do, we can slowly learn. These are some of the questions to ask ourselves.

What does this person mean to me? Do I like him or her? If not, how do I normally react to this person (or this type of person), and why?

If you can understand that you are always dealing with some aspect of your own nature represented by the people in your dreams, whether that aspect is conscious or not, the whole thing will make more sense. For example, you may dream about chasing a thief who has stolen your money. In recounting the dream you may be aware of how angry his action made you. You may recognize that something of value to you or to your well-being is being stolen. Perhaps some precious time is being wasted in the humdrum chores of life and this makes you resentful as you have little time for yourself; or more to the point, you are not organizing your time efficiently so that you *make* time for yourself. The masculine figure may well be representing this renegade masculine function of organization (or in this case disorganization) and you are being asked to value yourself more (guard the purse/money) and to handle your resources more carefully.

People We Know

Dreaming of people you know is a marvellous way of learning how to relate with more awareness. If you find yourself going through familiar feelings and reactions with people in your dreams, ask yourself: What does this person represent to me? What am I afraid of, attracted to, jealous of, angry with, needy for, critical of, etc. about this person? Let us say that you react to someone you know, for example your neighbour, in a critical way in your dream. You may need to face what it is in that person that you despise so much. It may be, for example, that you feel this person to be too self-effacing and timid, a bit of a 'doormat', and this makes you feel uncomfortable. Therefore you need to take back the energy you have projected on to your neighbour and ask yourself: Is there a part of me that I despise because *I* act in the very same way? Do I need to develop more autonomy and assertiveness in some area of my life? If this is not the case, then the converse may be true – perhaps you need to develop more deference or humility and cultivate a healthy respect for such values instead of denigrating them. In other words, you are reacting to a part of your own nature which you are projecting on to the dream character in order to reflect on your feelings about yourself. The nature of the projection will also be coloured, of course, by what your neighbour is doing during the dream.

When we dream of people whom we know in reality, our psyche chooses the characters in the dream scenario very carefully; this is because these characters do in fact exhibit particular qualities and feelings in reality, and they therefore make an impression on us. The way in which we interact with these people in the dream is an indication of how we are trying to become aware of those very same qualities and feelings in ourselves. For example, we may have a dream about being lost, and someone who we know to be helpful in our lives enters our dream to guide or support us. By defining which particular qualities we find positive in this person, we can then encourage ourselves to develop these qualities in reality in order to gain more clarity and control in our lives.

It is very important to remember also the gender of this person/ energy, as mentioned earlier. Is it a masculine energy – rationality, creative boldness, enterprise, courage and so on – or is it feminine energy – feelings, intuition, relatedness, sensitivity and the like – that is being shown to the dreamer through the dream figure?

We may find people in our dreams whom we know well or those whom we know only vaguely. We may incorporate into the story friends, lovers (past or present), royalty, film stars or enemies, but each one will play some aspect of our personality or inner nature according to the qualities that we attach to them. A client of mine, Fiona, had the following dream:

'My next-door neighbour was cutting holly in my garden. I came down the garden path and went inside my house to have coffee with her. The inside of the house seemed lower than my garden, so that as I looked through my window the lawn seemed to be raised higher than usual. Suddenly we heard a noise and we both looked around. My ex-husband was outside the window. He was being mischevious and was playing water through the hose-pipe on to the window-pane. Water poured down it like a sheet of rain, and it made us laugh.'

Fiona described her next-door neighbour as a woman who was much berated by her husband. She did not have a good self-image and was nervous, tense and watchful. Fiona happened to be working in therapy on her own low self-image and was learning how to value her strengths and talents. At the time of this dream she was very anxious about her financial circumstances and, although she had struggled up from a deprived childhood background to run her own successful business, nevertheless she still feared that all she had gained would be taken away from her. The neighbour, therefore, represented that aspect of her feeling-self that still plagued her.

The neighbour was cutting holly from Fiona's garden. In reality Fiona had witnessed this woman taking some holly from her garden without Fiona's consent in the past. This was typical of many instances when she had felt the effect of other people's lack of consideration, which reverberated back to a history of being and feeling abused in one way or another. Holly itself is a 'prickly' plant, not gentle to touch, and it described how Fiona felt when she was depressed. The depression is clearly illustrated by the low level of the house in relation to the lawn (not so in reality), and when Fiona was depressed she described herself as 'judgemental of others and critical of myself'.

However, both women were amused by the antics of Fiona's ex-husband. He represented the way in which she needed to channel her emotional energy, to introduce a note of lightness and play into her life which had become all too serious and burdensome. She had a lot more creative energy which she could release if she could just

transform her negative spiral of self-castigation into one of spontaneous action. She knew that there were many things that she could
do to earn more money without too much effort should she ever
need to, but her old fears kept holding her back. She described her
ex-husband as someone who 'had to put people down in order to
feel good'. This was exactly what she was doing to herself with her
own thought processes, and yet the dream was clearly showing her
another side of this man's nature – another approach that she needed
to take in order to lift herself out of the present situation.

It is not only *people* we know whom we dream of – but quite
often there are old familiar places that we visit. The age at which you
find yourself in the dream scenario will give you other clues about
unfinished business in the past or related to the past. A woman of
forty-four had the following dream:

'I'm in my childhood home and I'm about seven. I'm in one room
and my brother is in the other. He has a friend with him and they're
talking. I want to be with them but they are not aware of me. It does
not occur to me to ask to join them.'

This woman was in therapy with me, exploring the issue of what she
wanted to achieve in life. Her brother had been rather cruel to her
as a child and it had made her feel she was just a 'silly girl'. Neither
had she been valued as an intelligent person by her father, even
though she had now become a very intelligent and creative woman.
Consequently, she had a poor relationship to her feminine energy
and was still learning to identify her needs and gain confidence to
fulfil them. Because of her early experiences with her father and
brother she had a tendency to deny her own needs and undervalue
her talents. She had always wanted to be acknowledged by her
brother, but he did not want to play with her as a child. So now she
is learning to acknowledge and value her femininity and to nurture
her own inner child who is so full of potential. She went on to
release her feelings through a series of drawings and paintings, which
gradually became a work of love for her; this work was ideal as a
medium both of play and of expression of her inner creative wealth.

It is not always the case that you will be younger in your dreams,
but you may be, for example, holding a toy or sitting in a bedroom
that you had when you were eleven or fourteen, thus pinpointing a

certain stage of childhood that still needs some attention and which may be relevant in some way to your present circumstances. Part of our feeling nature can often be stunted or repressed at certain stages of development, or inhibited through our own experiences with other people. When the time is right, however, our psyche will give us all the clues we need in order to pick up where we left off and heal any wounds.

People We Don't Know

Sometimes, of course, we meet figures in our dreams whom we do not recognize at all. These figures will represent unknown aspects of our psyche with which we are being made familiar. They can be mystical and inspiring, or downright awful and threatening, but they are all aspects of ourselves that we need to understand.

One of my clients, Sheila, had a dream in which she was back at the school she attended between the ages of eleven and sixteen, but it had changed to a rather flimsy set of makeshift huts made of Formica. People told her that the school did not exist any more. She went into one of the huts and a woman whom she did not know was standing there with an ironing board. The woman acted very aggressively towards her, accusing her of using her iron and leaving it on. Sheila protested her innocence, saying that she had not been there for fifteen years, but the woman called her a liar. Sheila told her that she could prove it, and then she tried to threaten the woman physically just before she woke up.

In waking life Sheila was working very intensively on her early childhood. She had developed breast cancer and had recently undergone a mastectomy. This was the trigger for her to take her feeling life seriously and come to terms with a number of past hurts that she had not acknowledged. In the process, through therapy and dream-work, she discovered a few sub-personalities (independent parts of the whole personality that have somehow become split off and often polarized against each other) in her repertoire who were warring. The woman with the iron in the dream was the emergence of one major sub-personality which she subsequently called the Tyrant.

The Tyrant had become a very strident female, almost masculine in her deployment of power. She represented that part of Sheila who symbolically flattened the more artistic and sensitive part of her own femininity that had been so carefully engendered at her first educational establishment, a ballet school. As a child she had very much needed approval from her father, who did not value her artistic and sensitive nature. Because she did not get this approval, Sheila internalized this critical and rational aspect of her father's personality and she structured her life in such a way that too much stress and too many self-imposed pressures took their toll on her health. When I asked Sheila what ironing meant to her, she said it was a complete waste of time and she hated it. It emerged that she had also wasted a lot of time obeying this tyrannical side of herself, which demanded strength, intelligence, ambition and status.

The dream demonstrated how Sheila was still denying having anything to do with the iron (pressures and inhibitions internalized from her father) and was clearly angry at having to own up to this. The fact that the school was made up of flimsy Formica huts suggests that this period of her life was not very meaningful to her, and she had even tried to blot it out of awareness. However, her psyche encouraged her to look again at this time by introducing an inner character who could wake her up.

Whenever there is such a dominant sub-personality ruling the show it is important to ask where the other aspects of that person's nature have gone, as a polarity will always be set up when a sub-personality becomes dominant. Sometimes that polarity, or inferior aspect, will be evident in the dream and sometimes it may be necessary to explore it in other ways. In this instance Sheila was able to use Gestalt to identify that part of her nature that had needed to go underground. She called this sub-personality the Mouse, and it contained those spiritual characteristics that had been banished through disapproval and which had been too weak and vulnerable to emerge. The Mouse was desperately struggling for survival and was getting fed up with being criticized for her existence. Eventually, by allowing these two characters to dialogue, Sheila was able to change her lifestyle considerably to allow time and space for the Mouse's healing energies.

Some of our unconscious internal figures may be other-worldly characters from myth, fairy tale or religion. If they are all treated with the same respect and attention they will reveal their significance. The dreamer needs to explore his or her indentification with, or reactions to, the figure and so explore what is trying to be 'born' within. Some of these more numinous figures may connect the dreamer with an awareness and creativity that help him or her to transform a life situation or attitude, providing fresh insights and renewed energy which seem to come as if from nowhere.

Claire had been seeing me for several months in order to deal with her feelings of inadequacy as a mother and her bad self-image generally. Much of Claire's negative attitude towards herself and her lack of confidence stemmed from a rather rigid upbringing. She was not very well grounded in that she was not able to trust her instincts; she had a poor body-image and found difficulty expressing her sexuality freely. Matters were compounded by her being exiled from her country of origin because of political activities.

Claire worked through her pain and sense of loss by using imagery and poetry. She learned to nurture her inner child and slowly began to release her inner martyr from the cross of self-punishment. One day she brought in the following dream:

'I'm in my home with a friend and my cat, Baggins. There was a Gonk-like creature there also. [She later referred to it as a 'Glook'.] Its head and body were not distinct and it had no arms or legs. It was very shaggy and I was mainly aware of its eyes. It moved all over the place of its own volition and was very absorbing to watch because it had a lovely aura. It was friendly and joyful and emanated joy, comfort and lightness. It was peaceful and yet it was fun; it was rather like an alien. It played with the cat – almost flirted. I became concerned about the creature then – it was very vulnerable and might be ruptured [by the cat]. It could explode or shatter and then all its purity and innocence would be threatened.'

The dream occurred at a time when Claire had finished a rather unhappy relationship and was beginning a new one, which again brought up anxieties about trust and being vulnerable and intimate. As we worked on the dream with active imagination, it was clear that the Glook was representing Claire's emerging, yet still unconscious and primitive, sense of innocence and joy. Claire felt deeply protective towards this embryonic and trusting force within her and was quite worried that it (she) would be harmed once her instinctual nature (the cat) became aroused again. However, the Glook's joy and innocence *was* its own protection and Claire was worrying unnecessarily. In fact, the Glook was an aspect of her inner child seeking expression after having been inhibited for so long.

Using active imagination on the dream, she made the following observation: 'It moves all the time. It's excited, happy, inquisitive and gregarious. When I'm anxious about the cat, the Glook becomes nervous too but it tells me that it has strong fur and skin and it is magical; it has power.'

This creature therefore has a strong sense of its strengths and physical attributes. It certainly knew it was quite safe. I asked Claire to hold the Glook and see if any changes took place. Still using imagery, she reported that the Glook slowly began to grow arms. Claire was also aware that her breathing had changed to a deeper level and had become more rhythmical. The Glook then went back to playing, which Claire found relaxing to watch. It finally performed a few jumps and sprouted legs! The Glook had found its feet and the energy was grounded within Claire.

This 'magical' power of the Glook identifies the creature as an inner transformational symbol. Claire's contact with it, and therefore her recognition and integration of this inner power and spontaneity within her, made it a more conscious aspect of her personality represented by its taking on a more human form. Its power became her power, and the reality of the integration manifested physiologically as well as emotionally, which is a sign that Claire had found a touchstone for her real self at last. Such transformative dreams are usually of a healing nature.

It is also interesting to note the timing of this dream, which came almost nine months after Claire first entered therapy. The energy and confidence that this gave her enabled her to terminate therapy shortly afterwards and to begin a new cycle in her life with more strength and certainty. She has since established a new career for herself and her relationships with her partner and her daughter are more harmonious. Her story illustrates the fact that we are all like sleeping gods who are slowly having our power revealed to us, if we could only realize it and respect the process of dreaming.

SUMMARY

- There are usually two kinds of people in dreams — those you know and those you do not know.

- Your psyche chooses the people because of their specific characteristics and attitudes, which will be reflections of your own.

- There will be both men and women in your dreams. Male figures will be saying something about your relationship to your masculine energies, e.g. goal-directedness, will, rational thoughts and activity. Female figures will be saying something about your relationship to your feminine energies, e.g. feelings, moods, intuition and nurturing.

- If you want to understand why a certain person is in your dream ask: What does this person mean to me? Do I like him or her? If not, how do I normally react to him or her (or this type of person) and why?

- Take responsibility for whatever you are projecting on to that person and learn how to accept what they are teaching you about yourself. They may be showing you that you need to become more like them, or less like them; or you may just need to listen to what they have to say.

- You may find yourself interacting with someone in a scene from the past. This may give you clues about the origins of your present attitudes or behaviour.

- Sometimes we dream of characters whom we do not recognize. They will usually represent aspects of your psyche that are yet to be developed and integrated, or aspects of yourself to which you have not been paying attention. These characters can be dialogued with, using Gestalt or active imagination.

- Some unknown figures may be taken from myth, fantasy or religion. They are all illustrating the amazing dimensions and untapped possibilities of our psyche, and may lead us to inner transformation.

CHAPTER 11

The Shadow

I AM SURE THAT everyone who is interested in their dream world can bring to mind at least one dream where they have been chased by a threatening 'presence'. Sometimes the 'presence' is recognizable, and sometimes it is just a vague feeling, but usually the sense of fear and threat is very real.

It is amazing to think that we could run away so fervently from some aspect of our own psyche, but the fear is often of the unknown. The resolution comes however when we can turn round to face the pursuer, and be prepared to integrate the split-off energy into our consciousness. This is often the central theme of many fairy-tales passed on by oral tradition from generation to generation – a clue that we have all been running away since the beginning of time! Beauty has to learn to love the Beast and the Princess must kiss the frog before the mystical transformation and union can take place.

Jung called the hidden, repressed and unacceptable or nefarious aspects of the presonality the Shadow. Very often the Shadow contains powerful potential which, when fully integrated, can lead a person to maturity since much of that potential is still trapped in the unconscious state of infancy or childhood. In mythology the hero represents the conscious ego who must slay the dragon or monster (Shadow/fears) in order to achieve his goal or quest. Much that has been labelled 'evil' is pinned on to the Shadow, but it is important to recognize the 'pearl of great price' that is discovered in the transformation of the Shadow – which, after all, is only the distorted manifestation of natural instincts and creative impulses. The aim, therefore, is to stop running away from our unlived life and to turn round and embrace the energy.

Very often, because our Shadow is the result of primitive and

unconscious energy, it will appear in our dreams as a dark, primitive form – a hooded man or woman, a black animal or person, a savage beast, a primitive figure or simply a vague and threatening presence. Because it is our Shadow and unconscious, it may appear behind us, chase us or simply enter the scene and take us unawares because of its apparently alien or anarchic nature. For example, if a person has spent his or her life being neat, responsible and organized, the unlived or Shadow aspect of this person would probably manifest in the dream as a spontaneous, untidy and unfocused character such as a tramp or a 'crazy' person. This dream figure would no doubt make the dreamer or dream ego rather uncomfortable and yet would have a lot of valuable wisdom to offer. Very often the Shadow is the same sex as the dreamer. A client called Jane had the following dream:

'I am with a lot of people, "anarchist-types"; they have no order in their lives. I didn't like it but my husband did; it felt chaotic. They were all in my house. I then saw water tumbling down the stairs. Someone had left the bath running and I rushed up the stairs in a fury. There was a black girl there, not wearing very much. She was very laid back. The bathroom door was closed and she had run the bath. There were snooker tables all around and the black girl picked up a snooker cue and threatened me with it. I was frightened and went downstairs. Someone said there was a bomb in the house and everyone was to go outside.'

This client is a woman who was quite self-critical and who felt unacknowledged by family and friends. She had a lot of self-control and had lost touch with the ability to trust in her feminine sense of 'knowing', but despite this she spent a lot of the time in our initial sessions in floods of tears. Not surprisingly, issues of control or the lack of it come up in this dream, in which the sense of anarchy is set in her own home or sense of self. This was one of her greatest fears, a chaotic state, and yet her feelings were exactly that.

The water tumbling down the stairs in her psyche directed her attention to the need for a free flow of feelings, which in this case issued from the bathroom – a place of cleansing and healing. The Shadow is personified, in this dream, by a black girl whom Jane described as 'negligent, unstructured and disorganized', the very opposite to herself. The black girl is a primitive but very vital figure who, instead of brandishing a spear, threatens Jane with a snooker cue, The cue is symbolic of Jane's masculine power of control, which is being used destructively against herself instead of for playing with in the game of life in a creative and focused way. One could say that she was being 'snookered' by her own negative masculine energy!

Jane dialogued with this inner figure using imagery; the black girl said that she was angry with Jane for not cooperating with her, but for judging her instead. The girl knew the water was overflowing, but she did not care. She wanted Jane to open the door at the bottom of the house and let the water flow through, so that she could have some fun. Reluctantly, Jane did this; then the black girl put down her snooker cue and went in to turn off the tap, laughing. There was some sort of cooperation now, and Jane realized she was allowing her own tensions and frustrations to build up to a point at which she had to release them regularly through crying, although the crying did not really make her feel much better. What she really needed, therefore, was to acknowledge her feelings and to find a creative outlet or means of release.

In further dialogues with this character Jane was able to learn from her vitality, warmth, solidness, joy and the ability to go with the flow of life, which meant that some real and safe outlet could be given to her own damned-up feelings. In allowing her own latent qualities free expression Jane was giving herself permission to reclaim her body and instincts and trust her creativity. Eventually this energy was grounded when Jane set up her own practice in homeopathy and also found a creative outlet through dance, music and rearing animals. (It is worth noting that the threatened bomb scare in the dream did not worry the black girl at all. She was sufficiently in touch with her inner 'knowing' to sense that it was not based on fact, and she helped Jane to trust her gut reactions too!)

Because of the powerful and insistent nature of the unconscious aspects of the psyche, the Shadow is often the main character in recurring dreams, especially those which may have first surfaced in childhood when the child lived in a more numinous state of instinctual and unintegrated energy. Recurring dreams will be explored in more detail in Chapter 12; suffice it to say here that these early childhood nightmares often depict some aspect of the child's family Shadow – elements of unconscious instinctual energy that were being repressed by one or more members of the family and which the child elects to internalize and assimilate. Being a part of that family or collective psyche, the child will share the same complexes to some extent and will have the challenge of making these complexes conscious in later life. If the child-as-adult is able to undertake this work consciously and willingly, then in resolving and integrating the Shadow material personally he or she will also be healing the family wound. This often results in on-going, positive changes in the family dynamics.

Nightmares might recur in childhood, but the same themes may haunt us well into adulthood. As we mature and consciously face more of our fears we may resolve the dream or the story-line, and dream figures may change slightly as we develop and come to terms with different aspects of the root fear. As children, for example, we may have a recurring dream about being chased by a lion. As we get older, the energy of the lion (passion, lust, brute force) may become more modified and integrated through life's experiences, and will emerge later in a less primitive form in dreams. The energy may subsequently appear as a bully or a lusting man or woman, and if we can work with this powerful figure it may then transform yet again into, for example, a pushy boss or a tyrant. Eventually, if the character is communicated with, he or she may have some useful advice and energy to offer to the dreamer; and the dreamer may then start to accept and assimilate this split-off aspect, thereby gaining greater wholeness.

In dreams, as in the waking world, the Shadow serves to give us depth and character. Without it we are flat, two-dimensional beings; therefore integrating and working with the Shadow brings us more fully into the colourful spectrum of our lives.

SUMMARY

- The Shadow is often depicted in myth and fairy-tale as a loathsome person or creature that needs to be faced and vanquished – either through battle or through love.

- Jung called this part of us the Shadow, and it represents those aspects of our personality which are hidden, repressed or unacceptable to us in some way.

- Once accepted and integrated, the Shadow releases great potential for growth and healing.

- In our dreams it will often emerge as a primitive or dark form with an ominous or menacing presence. If it is a figure, it is usually the same sex as the dreamer.

- The techniques of Gestalt or active imagination can both be used to face and dialogue with the Shadow.

- With Gestalt, becoming and owning that Shadow part of yourself could be quite enlightening! Find out how it feels and what it wants from you.

- The Shadow may also be representing an aspect of your collective family Shadow – that part of the feeling nature which the whole family is suppressing.

- In most of our recurring nightmares the Shadow is the pursuer. We need to turn round and find out what we have been running away from. Then we can stop being the victim and start being the hero in our story of life.

CHAPTER 12

Recurring Dreams

V ERY OFTEN PEOPLE do not take much notice of their dream life. Many say that they do not have dreams when what they really mean is that they do not remember them. However, if there is a really important message that needs to be impressed upon us, the psyche uses repetition to drive the point home. This is the phenomena of the recurring dream, in which a particular sequence is enacted time and time again. The theme of such dreams is basically the same, although the scenario may differ slightly each time.

These kinds of dreams do tend to be remembered, as their content is usually either bizarre or emotionally charged. If the dream contains very anxiety-provoking material we call it a nightmare. People tend to remember these most of all, simply because they are often woken up at the point of crisis in the dream. Such dreams may be lifelong companions or they may disappear after so many years, usually at a point when the message has been assimilated and the dreamer has managed to deal with his or her feelings through various experiences in the world. For some people, long-standing recurring dreams are either so bizarre or so emotionally frightening that, either through curiosity or through anxiety, they seek some form of psychotherapeutic guidance. In fact, the 'cure' for such dreams is usually very simple and straightforward – the dreamer just needs to act on the message that the psyche is trying to convey.

The reason why we often tend to ignore recurring dreams is that many of us had them at some point during childhood. If they were pleasant we probably did not mention them – we just enjoyed them.

If they were unpleasant and we were afraid, we would probably have told our mother or father; the parent concerned would no doubt have told us that it was 'only a silly old dream' and then we would have been urged back to sleep. We soon got the message that we were being 'silly' to give the dream any kind of attention or significance.

Many adults, in fact, can still remember certain childhood dreams that captured their imagination and repeated a theme time and time again. Such dreams often retain their vividness and power many years later. My experience is that the childhood dream still remains embedded in our psyche, like a gift waiting to be unwrapped and used. It is often very simple and instinctual (many contain animals), and it can uncover the blueprint for our future growth and development. It is part of the myth by which we live. One man's childhood recurring dream was as follows.

'I was lost in a well-ordered forest. There were curved rides through it that were covered in snow. When I realized that I was lost and afraid, I was able to bring down a beautiful embroidered cloth saying "The End".'

The 'well-ordered forest' suggests that this child was living in a family that had a highly organized instinctual life, where the main basis for their reality was in ritualized activities, habits and behaviour patterns. The presence of the snow-covered rides suggests also that the feeling nature of the parents was quite controlled, so the child quite literally felt 'lost', with no real reference point for his unconscious energy and feeling nature to be integrated or contained. Like all children, he found a defence mechanism against the fear of such psychological abandonment; this was symbolized by the beautiful embroidered cloth which was brought down like the closing curtain of a play. Embroidery demands great attention to detail, and the child learned how to immerse himself in the intricate details of his own life in order to divert his greater sense of insecurity.

This man went on to become a craftsman involved in highly skilled but repetitive work, until a yearning for a deeper meaning to life and a need to relate more fully to his wife brought him into therapy. He could no longer 'pull the wool over his eyes', as it were. So here we can see how a childhood dream can serve as a message or blueprint for later adult life. Sometimes the message behind the dream gets resolved in childhood, but often, even if it stops recurring, the memory of it is lodged in our minds until such time as we can deal with it.

However, a recurring dream can begin at any stage in a dreamer's life. Some may come at regular intervals while others may reappear after a number of years, but there is usually a need for the dreamer to integrate some kind of experience, feeling or ability that as yet remains unresolved or unlived. Generally, the same theme will keep repeating with maybe a few variations until we discover its meaning. In my experience recurring dreams fall into two categories. There are some common themes which most of us have dreamt of at some time or another (I will mention a few later), and there are more personalized recurring dreams that may be unique to each dreamer.

One woman I know regularly dreams of driving her car but being out of control. She is usually driving downhill towards the sea, and sometimes she ends up in it. The accompanying feeling is often fear. In this particular instance, it related to the way that she felt about her self-control and sexual drives. As we talked through the dream it became clear that she feared being out of control yet her psyche continually directed her down into the unconscious, the sea, and the feeling realm. She related the sea to freedom and happiness, and therefore part of her wanted to lose control, while the other part felt that she ought to 'keep a hold on herself'. She tended to form a relationship with a man out of a sense of need, but then would feel 'smothered' if he demanded too much, because her freedom was also important to her.

As she comes to terms with this issue by taking responsibility for satisfying her emotional and creative drives in ways other than through partners – that is, by not depending solely upon men for her self-valuing – the dream will no doubt be modified each time. For example, she may find that next time she will be driving the car downhill to the sea in her dream, but it would then turn into a boat; she could learn to feel safe on the water without her needs taking her under in an unconscious manner. Or maybe she will find herself walking or cycling down to the water. As mentioned in Chapter 6, walking and cycling are the methods of transport that show the most autonomy. She might then find herself deciding to swim in the sea and enjoy the experience. Eventually, the dream will no longer need to repeat itself.

Other recurring dreams contain themes that we probably all recognize from time to time, such as the following:

Toilet dreams

In these dreams we are often trying to express either faeces or urine. We might be in an exposed place, which makes us feel very self-conscious, or perhaps we are always looking for an elusive toilet that we never seem to find! This kind of dream usually concerns the expression of creativity or self-assertion (faeces) or of the feeling nature (urine), or the inhibition of these. The question to ask ourselves if we are having such a dream is why are we afraid to 'let go' and express that which is natural to us?

Communication dreams

In these we are often trying to dial a number on a phone, for example, and not being able to get through; not being able to get the number dialled correctly; crossed lines, and so on. Here we need to ask who we are trying to communicate with, or which part of ourselves we need to contact. This kind of dream is about relating to something inside or outside of us.

Examination/test dreams

In these we are either back in an old exam or in a totally new setting, but not able to remember the facts that we need; having done no preparation or revision; going blank; running out of time; being the only one who does not know what to do, and so on. These kind of dreams often occur at times of trial in our life or when we put unnecessary pressures on ourselves. They often coincide with a time when we are entering a new cycle in our lives and we ask ourselves 'Will we cope?' and 'Do we know what we are doing?' There is often an authority figure within us somewhere who is being a bit of a taskmaster here, and this is all about trust, self-love and learning to pace ourselves realistically.

I am sure that all of us are familiar with at least one of these scenarios. These patterns may re-emerge at frequent intervals in order to prompt us to deal with the underlying psychic or emotional knot. Generally, then, recurring dreams occur because there is a matter of some importance that the psyche is urging us to attend to, and it uses repetition as a means of making sure that we attend to that message.

SUMMARY

- A recurring dream or theme often contains a particular scenario which is repeated time and time again.

- We often wake up at a point of crisis and never resolve the situation in the dream. Sometimes these dreams recur over many years.

- The dream challenges us to resolve and integrate some kind of experience, feeling or ability that we are anxious about.

- Once the symbolic significance of the theme is recognized we can begin to tackle the situation more constructively. We can re-enter the dream and change the way we react or carry through with a particular challenge or activity.

- Some themes are unique to us and others are common to many people – such as themes of communication, toilets and examinations.

CHAPTER 13

Listening to the Body Through Dreams

WE HAVE LOOKED at the way the dream uses the body as a metaphor. Now we are going to deal with the way the dream diagnoses the cause of physical illness or suggests ways to heal any bodily discomfort.

Nearly all physical illness has a psychological basis; this has been explored by many therapists over the last century. We are actually in the process of rediscovery, because our ancient ancestors had no difficulty with this concept. They understood that there is a basic energy that moves freely through us when we are in a healthy state, but that this energy can be blocked if we are stressed or unhappy in some way and may then manifest as illness or dis-ease.

The Chinese called this energy chi and developed acupuncture as a holistic system to harmonize the channels of the body, or meridians, and therefore to effect a change on all levels – physical, emotional and spiritual. In India this basic life energy was called kundalini or 'serpent power'; it too needed to flow through passageways, or nadis, and similarly it could be blocked at various levels in the body (called chakras) depending on the state of development of the individual and his or her disposition. Tantric exercises were developed in order to relate to this energy, as well as a system of exercises called yoga in which postures (asanas), breathing and meditation were brought to focus on this kundalini energy, the free flow of which enhanced an individual's sense of well-being, health and awareness. There was an acceptance that this special energy pervaded the body and had a life of its own that could also express itself in the dream. Eastern cultures, therefore, value the dream as a mirror of the activities of this energy, which is released from its physical vehicle during sleep.

In ancient Greece, Aristotle and Hippocrates noticed that dreams incorporated physiological sensations of the individual while asleep, and they felt that dreams could therefore be seen as useful predictions of the disease states before they actually manifested. However, Western thinking has separated the body from the soul since the time of the seventeenth-century philosopher Descartes. Modern physics has viewed the body as a product of specific mechanical parts with little or no room in it for a psyche, soul or unifying energy. Fortunately, the Gestalt psychologists of the late nineteenth century suggested that the body had a nature that was more than the sum of its parts. Freud added to this with his acknowledgement of psychosomatic states – in other words, that anxiety, fears or sexual inhibitions *did* affect the functioning of the body. Then Jung, more than any other practitioner, gave us back the validity of a vital part of our nature, the psyche or Higher Self, which sought recognition, acceptance and growth towards wholeness through the dream.

With reference to the body, Wilhelm Reich opened up the field of body/mind research more fully with his work on the nature of energy in living organisms. Reich was a psychoanalyst practising in the 1940s. In his own research into areas such as hysteria, he began to notice a correlation between the functional identity of a person's character and his bodily attitude or 'armouring' – his term for the chronic muscular tensions held within a person's body. Reich believed that if a person had experienced a sexual trauma in early childhood, that same trauma often became buried or repressed in later years. The repression also affected certain feelings and ideas, and the clamping down of these feelings would create the symptoms that presented eventually as illness.

This work was further developed by practitioners like Alexander Lowen, who created the therapeutic technique called bio-energetics. He defined bio-energetics as 'the study of the human personality in terms of the energetic processes of the body'. Using this method, muscular tensions were identified and released, and it would also release trapped aggression, anxiety or sexuality which were seeking integration. Certain exercises, combined with deep breathing, are used to discharge these repressed tensions, leading to a greater feeling of aliveness and connection with the body.

But more specifically, it is therapists like Arnold Mindell and Louise Hay who have developed the area of mind/body healing and brought it more fully into popular awareness. Louise Hay, after having understood her own emotional stresses and cleared her own body of cancer, and from the experience of working with many seriously ill clients, went on to compile her findings on the correlations of the mental/emotional causes of physical illness. She also teaches people how to heal their illness through understanding these emotional causes.

Arnold Mindell, an American Jungian analyst who developed what is known as Process Oriented Psychology, investigated the hidden significance of physical symptoms and discovered that the unconscious is speaking to us all through these physical symptons, as it does through our dreams in symbolic form. He used the word 'Dreambody' to describe 'a multi-channelled information sender asking you to receive its message in many ways'. He observed how this 'Dreambody' gave us vital clues about the source of our disease, with essential information appearing over and over again in dreams and body symptoms in order to capture our attention. Because of the mercuric nature of the body's energy, it needs a flexible and adaptable attitude to be able to 'read' body symptoms of illness or disease using whatever channel is being activated at the time, whether it be tone of voice, body language, dream work or language itself.

Let us look at a couple of examples of the way we can communicate with our own mind/body process through the dream.

A woman called Sarah had a dream in which she was in her parents' house. At one point in the dream her brother (who in reality is prone to bouts of schizophrenic behaviour) called her into his room and showed her something on the bottom of the curtain. When she bent down to look at it he put his hands around her neck. She could feel his strength but she could not shout out. She woke up feeling very frightened.

We did some work on this dream, I asked Sarah to identify where in her body she felt her brother's presence. She said it was in her solar plexus and throat. She felt threatened and could not shout. If she could have shouted, she would have given him an ultimatum – 'either to get out of the room or to change his ways'. She described her brother as out of touch with his body and mainly functioning through his intellect in a very intense way. She also felt he was sitting on a lot of violent feelings.

When we re-enacted the scene from the dream, I stood behind Sarah as she bent down and then put my hands round her throat as in the dream. When I asked her how she felt she described a pain in her shoulders and neck as though she was being pushed down while at the same time her throat was seizing up. 'It feels like a yoke on my back affecting all my bronchial tubes and draining all the life force out. I can't breathe, can't take in life or give it out.' (Sarah told me later that she had in fact suffered with bronchitis in the past.)

The most immediate thing that Sarah felt was the terror of really being in her own body and being fully alive (that is, breathing fully). Her brother was not really at home in his own body, and Sarah could see how they shared this feeling. She had come back into therapy to deal with issues related to her femininity and her feelings of lack of self-worth. As she bent down in this exercise with my hands round her throat, Sarah connected with a feeling of terror. I asked her what the terror was about. She replied, 'Terror about life. What does it mean to be fully in life? If I enter fully into life, I might be seen.' Curtains are also associated with hiding or blocking the light (even more so if you dream about blinds or shutters), and no doubt her psyche was getting Sarah to attend to the ways in which she hid from this issue.

So it seemed that Sarah was afraid to express herself openly and creatively. She was not given much opportunity to do so as a child, and she felt a lot of fear around it now. She had felt that her brother had received most of the attention in the family because of his condition, and so she had projected on to him part of the blame for her own stifled creativity. However, the whole family shared this suppression to some extent, and Sarah now needed to find a way to change the pattern for herself.

I requested her to ask the 'brother image' in the dream what he needed from her before he would release her. The brother image said, 'I want your attention and I want to be free.' Sarah was then able to hold the brother figure with love, and she gave him permission to be expressive and communicative. She was in fact giving permission for her wounded inner masculine creative energy (that part of her which could affirm and assert itself) to be healed. I then asked her what she would need to do physically to remove my hands from her throat. She said she would have to make Kung Fu movements, and she proceeded to raise her arms up and throw me off. Later on, in her own home, Sarah practised using her arms more energetically by throwing them up into the air as though releasing a burden. She realized that this action released her breathing also, and feelings of energy and anger surfaced which she was able to express by beating cushions, again with the emphasis on using her arms energetically.

Sarah learned through this simple amplification of the dream element that she needed to reaffirm her self-worth and her need to receive love. Arms are for holding and receiving the experiences of life. This cannot be done if anger is blocking the process. Sarah also became more aware of listening to the needs of her body for physical comfort, love and expression.

Another woman called Kay came into therapy; one of the main issues we were working on together was her relationship with her mother, which she felt was preventing her from making a good connection with her femininity. She had not felt supported or accepted by her mother except in a very conditional way. Kay was a sensitive and artistic woman who did not have much confidence in her own talents, and she felt at times that the world was against her. She had the following short dream:

'There was a big spider under the skin of my face and another one was jumping up and down in my room. I didn't like them being there.'

When I asked Kay what she felt about spiders in general, she said she was very frightened of them because they were ugly and moved so fast. I then asked Kay to put her hand where the spider was on her face and try to remember the sensation of it under the skin. She took a while to connect with the image, and then she remembered that she had had terrible acne on her face when she was a teenager. She had been teased about it and it had made her feel ugly.

Next, I asked Kay to talk to the spider using active imagination and ask it why it was there and what it wanted. The spider said it was getting life from her in a parasitic way. It also wanted to go on the other side. As Kay sat there, with a hand on each side of her face now, I asked her what that felt like. She replied that she did not actually mind the spiders being under her skin and cheeks now that she had talked to them. She would feed them, and in return they told her that they would fill out the natural hollows in her face. Before this dream, Kay had been concerned about her weight. When she first entered therapy she had just finished a relationship and was looking very gaunt and thin. It was interesting that soon after this particular dream she did begin to fill out, and many people who knew her had begun to notice a positive change in her appearance and her attitude towards her femininity. Kay also began to give herself the kind of recognition for her talents that she had not received from her parents and from her mother in particular.

It is also interesting that the spider is the archetypal symbol for the Great Mother in her terrible aspect of the weaver of destiny. Spiders often appear in dreams (and large ones in reality!) when we need to make some major decision over our personal destiny. Their unpredictable behaviour, like Fate, challenges us to take power into our own hands or render ourselves powerless. In this case, Kay decided to break the pattern of being labelled by others and create her own destiny. She chose to listen to her own instincts.

If you keep in mind that your dream is full of aspects of yourself, it will become easier to work at the body level; simply 'become' the element of the dream that you are curious about. If there is a bird singing on your shoulder in your dream, just explore what it feels like to become the dream bird for a while. If you can attempt to move and sing like the bird, even better. Talk to the dream bird and ask it what it wants from you. Through giving it a voice you will release the energy to flow through you, and in so doing, associations that your psyche is giving you will become clearer. It may well be, for example, that you would like to sing or use your voice in a more uninhibited way, and your dream bird is trying to awaken this aspect of your nature; or it may simply be an acceptance of joy and innocence in your life.

If you dream about a baby crawling on the floor, get down and crawl along the floor like the dream baby. See what it feels like to be so close to the earth, using your arms and legs in this very grounded and basic way. It might evoke feelings of safety or a sense of adventure; or it might even reconnect you to a sense of trust or achievement. Your body contains a multitude of memories and sensations waiting to be released, developed, and remembered. Again, re-enacting the dream sequence will help this release.

Sometimes it is useful to work on a dream with a friend. As in Sarah's dream, if you have dreamt of a particular episode where you were experiencing some kind of tactile sensation from a dream image or perhaps you were being pinned down or held back in some way, then ask your friend to apply or re-enact the same pressure or motion so that you are free to concentrate on the sensation in your body. Your friend can then ask you the following questions.

(1) What does this feel like?

(2) What does this remind you of?

(3) Is this (for example, being held back, pushed down, irritated, pressured and so on) happening to you in some aspect of your life now?

Take responsibility for the fact that you are allowing this to happen to you, and then decide what you need to do in your life to change matters. I think you will find that the impact of this kind of exercise is immediate and fun to explore.

SUMMARY

- Nearly all illness has a psychological basis. Through the centuries many approaches, such as yoga and acupuncture, have been devised to help people reconnect to their vital energy and clear any blocks to the flow of that energy system.

- These approaches were usually based on the understanding that human beings have spiritual, emotional, intellectual and physical aspects to their natures. All these aspects must be in balance for the person to be in a state of health. Blocks in one area can create blocks in other areas of the person's experience.

- Freud acknowledged psychosomatic states through his work with clients. He observed that anxiety, sadness and sexual inhibition did affect the functioning of the body.

- Other modern therapists such as Reich, Lowen, Mindell and Hay have all contributed more knowledge to this area.

- Identify the somatic clues that your dream gives you and use imagery to focus on a certain area of your body, describing the sensations more fully.

- These sensations and images will often take on a life of their own and show you what they need for their healing. You will also gain the necessary information about how your attitudes, beliefs and feelings are causing the physical sensations.

- Another technique is to give expression to the dream element that you are wishing to understand – for instance, if your leg is in spasm in your dream, then let your leg really kick out while you are awake. Find out what it wants to do and then ask 'Why?' Are you needing to express your anger or kick over the traces? It may be that you are inhibiting this urge.

- It is sometimes useful to have a helper present who can amplify the pressure or sensation on the appropriate part of your body. This can help you to focus more fully in order to make the necessary connections at the feeling level.

CHAPTER 14

The Language of Dreams

I AM CONSTANTLY AMAZED at the rich and fertile way in which our psyche can educate and amuse us through the language of dreams. Often it is only in the telling or writing down of the dream that we become conscious that the words we spontaneously use to describe the images or actions in our dreams are so revealing. Sometimes we are so unaware of the puns and descriptions we 'choose' that it has to be pointed out to us just how ingenious we are.

For example, one man described a scene in his dream thus: 'There was a furnace in a stone-walled room. . . .' On further examination it emerged that he had been very angry about a certain situation (the furnace is a container of fire or anger) but had not expressed his anger openly to anyone. He had 'stone-walled' it! This was no doubt how others had experienced him also.

A woman who described her dream as taking place 'in a board-room' suddenly became aware as she said this that her job was not stimulating enough and that she wanted to make some dramatic changes. A boardroom is a place where people such as examiners or directors of a company meet to make decisions – apart from the obvious pun on boredom.

In another dream, a woman found herself on a Greek island called Scard; in reality she knew of no such island. Although she was supposed to be on holiday in the dream, she was unable to relax because of constant worries about needing to work or to carry out certain duties at home. After some discussion it became quite clear that she was too 'scared' to relax and enjoy herself, and she needed to learn

how to slow down a bit. In view of the fact that she had never been to Greece before, the psyche may even have been punning on the fact that relaxing and enjoying herself were beyond her comprehension or 'all Greek to her'.

Dreams pun on words, names and also on everyday phrases and colloquialisms. One man dreamed that he had learnt to play a very complicated piece on the trumpet. Everything was fine until he had to play in front of an audience, and then he played badly. In reality, this man did not play any musical instrument. However, he was not very good at expressing his views to others or asserting his needs. The dream was telling him that he had the potential to 'blow his own trumpet' and that he needed to practise being forthright with other people.

Sometimes it is in speaking and describing the dream that the connections become apparent. A man was describing the opening scene of his dream to me: 'It's a grey day and I'm on top of a hill, but it's not grass − it's made of concrete.' When I asked him to describe the hill he replied that it was more like a hump. I then asked him if he 'had the hump' about anything, and he admitted feeling depressed (grey) and annoyed about a certain situation in his life which we then talked about. The fact that the dream had created a man-made construction in an otherwise natural environment suggested that the dreamer had to break down some long-standing emotional and intellectual defences before he could change the 'climate' of his feelings. In fact, the rest of the dream went on to show him how to come to terms with his feelings.

Dreams are very good at incorporating the language of the body, which can be very amusing when you appreciate the references. We all quite instinctively use phrases based on our physiological experiences: we 'give someone the elbow', we have our 'back against the wall', we 'toe the line' or we 'can't stomach' something. Be aware of your psyche directing you in this way. If, for example, you dream that you cannot move your head, are you being 'stiff-necked'? If you are losing your hair in a dream, is there something making you anxious or annoyed so that you need to 'keep your hair on'? Perhaps you dream about carrying a heavy load or a large rucksack, and your psyche is really telling you to stop shouldering heavy burdens in your life. You may even develop shoulder problems in your physical reality.

The last point is important because, as we discovered in Chapter 13, our dreamlife plays a vital role in healing not only our emotional and mental nature but also our physical self. Very often we are given clues in the dream about the kinds of pressure or conflict that are building up within us. Sometimes these clues come in the form of physiological references or body language. If we work with these references we can often prevent or cure any disharmonies which might or do emerge at the physical level. If we ignore these references, then nature may well attempt to restore the balance through manifesting physical symptons or disease.

So language, and puns in particular, can be overlooked if you do not scan the dream for meaning at all levels. It is quite clear that our psyche does have a sense of humour, even if we do not credit our personalities with that quality!

SUMMARY

- Dreams often use certain situations and words with humorous effect. In recounting our dreams we can sometimes discern the significance of double-entendre.

- Certain activities which we find ourselves doing in dreams may be metaphors, describing certain attitudes or behaviour, e.g. 'blowing your own trumpet', 'making your bed and lying in it', 'getting on your high horse' etc.

- Puns on words are very common. If you cannot see the significance of a certain name or word that has been used in your dream, try to see it in a different context and use some lateral thinking.

- Names of people and places are often invented in dreams, but they may well be composites of other words or names which are of significance in your life and which may give a clue about what the dream is telling you.

- Parts of the body may be used to describe forms of behaviour that you are acting out in the reality of your waking life, e.g. 'giving someone the elbow' or 'cold shouldering' someone.

- Often, the significance of such word-play in dreams will not be apparent until the dream is either recorded or related to someone afterwards.

CHAPTER 15

Birth Dreams

DURING THE COURSE of a life we go through many cycles and times of transformation. New roles and experiences need to be accommodated while old habits and redundant value systems have to be shed if we are to continue to develop as whole human beings. At these key times, the themes of birth and death will often appear in our dreams and, unless an actual birth is imminent or a death has been sensed through precognition, these themes are to be taken not literally but symbolically.

Births occur at times when we are bringing forth new aspects of ourselves. They are more common in the dreams of my female clients as they get in touch with the spontaneous, trusting core of their being through psychotherapy and inner work such as guided imagery. However, men too may dream of an 'inner' woman giving birth, representing some new creative dimension of themselves coming to fruition.

As we learn to trust our intuition and instinctual self we will release more creative energy which will inspire us to take up new interests, hobbies or directions in life. These will often manifest as the birth of children in our dreams. We will be given clues as to how prepared we are for the births, and how able we are to nurture and sustain these new shoots of creativity. We will also gain insight into the nature of our 'inner children', some of whom can miraculously age several years within the first few minutes of birth.

A woman called Joanna, who had been in therapy for a couple of weeks, had the following dream:

'I'm in a strange hospital. It is mostly serving mothers and children; the children are in pushchairs. The mothers and children are out-

doors, all in rows, on a slope. I'm a patient there, but I seem to be wearing a nurse's uniform. I'm starting to bleed from the vagina. A nurse comes along to see if I'm pregnant and she takes a sample of urine to check me. I'm thinking: "Hang on, I've had a hysterectomy – so who's baby is this? Which lover was the father? No wonder I've been feeling fat!" I then find myself with my child among the mothers and babies in rows outside.'

Joanna was in therapy to develop a more positive self-image and to explore a new direction in life after separating from her husband. She had a lot of creative energy that needed channelling, but she often lacked confidence in herself and this would cause her to give up on various ventures that she started. She used to be a nurse, and she found nursing exciting. Now she was starting a new cycle in her life and had set up as a masseuse. In the dream she was wearing her old nurse's uniform which she associated with a feeling of power and authority, qualities that she certainly possessed. But this time she was a patient – in other words she was back in a vulnerable position at this new stage in her life. The beginning of any new cycle in life is bound to be a heady mixture of exciting potential and fear of the unknown.

But Joanna was developing new aspects of herself through this challenge. Out of the sadness and break-up of the marriage, she was learning to nurture herself and was discovering her own strength and resourcefulness. In the dream she could not work out how she had become pregnant. Part of her had not really been prepared for the way her marriage had ended, and she still mourned its passing. She was not totally ready for the reality of her new existence.

She also did not know who the lover was, and later she described the birth in the dream to me as 'immaculate', especially as she had had a hysterectomy in reality. 'But then,' she said, 'I do consider all birth as immaculate in that birth *is* so magical.' Certainly, dream births appear immaculate. Very often the dreamer finds herself pregnant and giving birth without any notion that a partner was involved. This is because the dream baby is the result of an alchemical process within, a balancing of the male and female energies that results in a new element of creativity being born.

When Joanna went back into the dream in guided imagery she

was aware that she was very much a spectator. After the birth she was with the other mothers and children, but they did not take any notice of her. Her own inner child very quickly aged about three or four years and sat on her knee. The child told her that the mothers were frightened because Joanna was wearing her uniform. She also found out that all the children were waiting for operations on their mouths and they were in rows to keep things tidy. They were outside the hospital because the building had not been finished yet.

As we talked about this afterwards, Joanna reflected on how the uniform probably represented the persona which she presented to the world. She could give the impression that she was in control and had things worked out, but in reality she was afraid to reveal her vulnerability. She later joined a women's group and allowed her defences to come down in a safe environment. Her early childhood experience had been one of rejection and criticism; learning to trust that she was lovable, warts and all, in the eyes of others, was very important to her now as an adult.

The children were kept in rows for tidiness, indicating the kind of controls that Joanna was imposing on her spontaneity. They were all waiting for operations on their mouths. The mouth is the place where we take in nourishment but it is also our means of communication. To Joanna, the mouth meant words and expressing herself. As a child she had felt that no one really took the time to listen to what she said, and it had left her feeling that no one would like what she said now. She had wanted to write a book, but felt afraid to start in case people thought she was a 'know-all'.

The birth of Joanna's inner child represented a growing awareness of the new ways in which her budding creativity needed to be given expression. The sex of the child will often indicate the kind of energies that need to be encouraged (see Chapter 10, on the qualities of the masculine and the feminine). Also, as mentioned above, these inner babies will often age rapidly within the dream. The age of the child can be an indicator of the point at which a person began a new cycle or creative project in their life; for instance, you may give birth to a six-month-old baby and then, looking back, find that six months earlier was when you first conceived an idea to start writing a book or to embark upon a new direction in life. ('Conceived', in this context, means the first manifestation or expression of an idea or project rather than 'conception' as in the moment of pregnancy.) In Joanna's case the child was about three or four years old; three or four years earlier was about the time that she began a new cycle of exploration and spiritual searching before her marriage broke up. This new dimension of her awareness still needed very careful nurturing and guidance before it was fully integrated, and it had certainly generated a lot of self-growth and learning. By giving the inner child an age, the psyche is reassuring you that the creative impulse you have generated is alive, healthy and growing apace!

Things to be aware of in birth dreams therefore are:

(1) The sex and age of the baby.

(2) The conditions of the birth – was it easy, painful or were you not aware of the process?

(3) Were there helpers around at the birth – that is, what qualities did you need to draw upon for this new awareness to emerge?

(4) Does the baby have any physical problems that need special attention and healing? Remember that dreams will give clues about the area which we are blocking by using the body as a symbol (see Chapter 13).

Finally, if the child is born sickly or weak, do not forget to feed it! Another client of mine, Hannah, came into therapy to explore how she could break out of a lot of negative patterns that she had established over the years. She had been a victim of incest as a child and had continued to abuse herself throughout her life by drinking heavily, self-harming and having a series of sexual affairs that had left her feeling even more confused and lacking in self-worth.

Hannah had a series of dreams in which babies figured as a central theme. When she first came into therapy she dreamed that she was put in charge of a baby but did not know what to do with it. The baby was only six inches long and she described it as 'all purply-red and ugly'. Although she did give it a bottle and laid it down to sleep, the baby had no clothes on and Hannah put it in a metal supermarket basket with nothing to lie on. When the baby stuck to the bottom of the basket Hannah panicked and had to peel it off the metal.

This dream illustrates the way Hannah's feelings were neglected and abused through her experiences in life. We had to use guided imagery to go back into the dream and clothe, feed and love the baby. Through this act she recognized that she did not need to stay wounded and that she could empower herself to heal the neglected baby/feelings within.

In a subsequent dream, Hannah had a baby boy. But her mother said that Hannah could not look after it because she was not responsible enough; she could only visit it. Hannah tried to confront her mother in the dream, but was eventually beginning to doubt if she really *was* able to be a good mother herself. This dream was dealing with Hannah's emerging will and individuation. It came at a stage when she was breaking up with a partner and trying to set some boundaries and goals for herself. She had always tended to live life vicariously through others but was now needing to develop her own sense of self and direction. This emerging aspect of her, the baby boy, was being held captive by her mother. In reality, Hannah had felt some rivalry between herself and her mother. It was an uneasy relationship in that Hannah had been conscious of how much of her own creative energy had been tied up in rebelling against her mother, as if to punish her for not being supportive or receptive when she needed her. She recognized that she had never really asked how she could use her own creative energy in a positive way to support herself, and that she was still living out this rebellion with her mother at an unconscious level.

Again, using guided imagery, Hannah went back into the dream and reclaimed the baby boy as her own, thus taking back her power and autonomy and releasing her creativity from the negative mother within. This act was another positive step away from her 'victim' stance. It was necessary for her to feel safe in order to make her own goals in life, as her relationship with her partner was dissolving.

And so we can see that the birth of these inner energies as dream babies is a very timely event in our psychological development. We do not have to respond to the new arrivals with guided imagery as I have outlined in these examples: these babies will grow and flourish whether or not we intervene. But guided imagery can speed up the process and make it more conscious. The important thing to remember is that an inner birth is as much of a cause to celebrate as birth on the outer levels of reality – and not nearly as painful or expensive!

SUMMARY

- Dream births occur at times when we are starting to manifest new aspects of ourselves.

- New interests or projects, the growth of inner potential or a new direction in life will often be symbolized by the birth of a baby in your dreams.

- We will often be shown how prepared we are for these 'births' and how able we are to nurture and sustain this new creative potential.

- If you have dreamt of neglecting an inner baby or if the baby is taken away from you or is sickly in some way, you can use guided imagery to go back into the dream and react differently or ask relevant questions.

- Dream babies may age rapidly within a short time of birth. The age of the child can be an indication, by tracing backwards, of when a new cycle or creative project was first begun or conceived.

- Be aware of the age and sex of the baby. What were the conditions of the birth? Was it painful or were you unaware of the birth? Who was present or helping you? Is the baby sickly, precocious or unusual in some way?

- Whether or not we act on the dream using guided imagery, these dream babies will grow and develop as potential within us and will eventually manifest in some way on outer levels.

CHAPTER 16

Death Dreams

I**T IS PERHAPS** a sobering thought that during the course of living we are constantly dying. In order to make room for new awareness, we must be willing to let go of old and outworn attitudes, behaviour and values. We are constantly undergoing a process of transformation, even down to the sloughing off of old skin cells as new ones take their place. Death, therefore, needs to be understood as a process of transformation and in dreams the death of a character should not be cause for alarm (only in exceptional cases are such dreams precognitive).

One of my clients, Carol, had a very short dream which turned out to be longer than she imagined!

'I'm carrying a coffin with some men through a crowd of men. There is a dead man inside and we are struggling to get through the crowd.'

This dream was one in a series of dreams containing men as the main characters. In the previous week Carol had been talking about the fact that she felt there was a frustrated exhibitionist inside her – a 'loud and physical warrior'. Her psyche had certainly focused quite specifically on masculine energy in this dream. As we talked about it, Carol said she carried the coffin on her right (masculine) shoulder and she remembered the struggle to get through the crowd of men. We decided to go through this, albeit short, dream with guided imagery.

When she relived the dream Carol was very aware of the relief of eventually getting through the crowd. She decided to look into the coffin to see who the man was. She discovered that he was not an old man, as she had first thought, and that he seemed to be curled up inside the coffin. At this point, going more deeply into the dream had activated a flash of memory as another part of the dream was retrieved from her subconscious. She remembered being in her ex-husband's house where there were quite a lot of people. A man (who she felt was the man in the coffin) was getting angry and throwing something like acid into people's eyes. He had then been caught by some other people and bound to a stick in a foetal position. When Carol asked the man why he was so angry he replied that he was frustrated at people because they were not really 'seeing' him. She helped to untie him and he stood up. He told her that he needed to be acknowledged.

Talking afterwards, Carol said she recognized the man as her own creative energy. When she was young she remembered moving with her parents to a Greek island, where she lived a life of relative freedom and spontaneity. She was beginning to blossom as an adolescent and show an interest in boys, but she felt that her parents found her emerging adolescent energy too much to deal with. At the age of fourteen she was sent off to live with a family in Germany. This was a very claustrophobic experience for her after the instinctual life she had been living in Greece. The family were strict and inhibited, with strong religious and moral values. She felt she had to 'sit on my spirit' and repress a lot of her natural exuberance, and she began to feel 'fat, ugly and a misfit'.

A lot of her instinctual energy had had to go underground, but was emerging now in the form of this dream character who needed acknowledging and who was throwing the acid of his frustrated feelings into people's eyes. If they were not going to acknowledge him, he would damage them. He was then tied up to the stick in a foetal position, symbolizing the way Carol felt bound by the rules and inhibitions that she had experienced as a young girl.

This frustration also emerged in her relationship with her partner, who she felt was 'not available emotionally'. She turned her anger on herself and became self-critical, feeling 'second-rate and a problem'. In fact, Carol needed to get back in touch with this wild, creative energy and feel safe with it again. She had always attracted partners who were quite ambitious and work-oriented, whereas she herself felt as though she was not achieving anything in her life. In setting her inner man free and releasing him from his critical, rule-bound beliefs, she was giving herself permission to express her spontaneity and revive that part of her that she called her 'frustrated exhibitionist'. She said that she loved to make a lot of noise and to be physically unfettered, and she recognized her need to explore dance, drama and other forms of self-expression. Perhaps, in releasing all this creative energy, Carol would begin to feel alive again and finally get in touch with a sense of her own power and ambition.

Death in dreams, therefore, often symbolizes the need to let go of some aspect of ourselves that is holding us back from growing as individuals. Such inner growth can be frightening, because we are never quite sure what will replace our 'old selves'. Will our 'new selves' be any better? The fear of the unknown can make us panic, and that panic can often manifest in dreams as someone close being taken away from us through death. But we need to look carefully at the characteristics and behaviour that this person represents within us before we can understand what we are being asked to relinquish.

Rachel had the following dream.

'My younger sister, Sheila, was dying. She couldn't move her limbs. She wasn't dead but I was crying about this. She was preparing to float off but she said she would come back to say goodbye to me.'

Rachel described Sheila as more solid and down-to-earth than her, but also as unimaginative and superficial. Rachel recognized that Sheila represented those aspects of her own nature which were controlling and rigid (her sister in the dream could not move her limbs). She feared letting go of this side of her because she might then find that her uninhibited, adventurous energy would come to the fore and take over (threat of the new).

Again, it was not by chance that this dream came after a session when we had been talking about Rachel's awareness of the split in her nature. She had begun to label her 'controller' as the 'Boring One' who 'was ill, did not feel like dancing, moaned, was rigid, studious and concerned with time'. It was not that Rachel's sister epitomized all these negative qualities, but rather that the psyche chose a 'fit' who was close enough in some ways and would be sufficiently linked to Rachel that she would feel and remember the attachment and loss.

We decided to deal with this by using Gestalt to heal the split. Rachel's 'Boring One' dialogued with her 'Exciting One' and, through integrating the best of both, she found an ideal third energy which could hold the balance and enable her to move on to a new way of experiencing life. The fact that Rachel's sister was preparing to die and would come back to say goodbye suggested that Rachel was being given plenty of time to make this transition and would probably be allowed more than one opportunity.

Sometimes, however, there are aspects of ourselves which we have to rescue from death or extinction; perhaps we have not nurtured them enough, or we may feel unworthy in some area of our being. It is important, therefore, to recognize the difference between that which we must relinquish and that which we must retrieve. Elaine brought this dream to therapy.

'I decided I was going to die. My mother was preparing the funeral arrangements. She prepared food and flowers. I then said, "I don't want to die any more." But my mother said, "You'll have to now, I've prepared everything." '

This dream was illustrating Elaine's growing awareness of her own individuality as she began to take a stand against her mother. She had described her mother as quite dominant and controlling, a fact which she became more aware of as therapy progressed. Her mother placed a lot of importance on material things, and Elaine had realized how this emphasis had prevented her from getting in touch with her inner realm of feelings, instincts and intuition. She realized that this block on her feelings was restricting her work as an artist. In her marriage, also, she recognized that she had chosen a partner who, she felt, was restricting her emotionally and who was unable to understand her need to explore her psyche through therapy.

In the dream Elaine had made the decision to die, or cut off from her conscious awareness of life, and escape into the unconscious realm of oblivion. Like the mother who was controlling the proceedings, Elaine was existing on automatic pilot – getting things done, but detached from any meaning or purpose to her actions. Then, for whatever reason, she decided to change her mind and live. Her decision to follow her impulse for life and autonomy immediately brought resistance from the internalized controller/mother. When she went into the dream Elaine realized how angry she was at her mother's resistance to her claiming back her right to live. 'I'm worth more than flowers and food!' she exclaimed as she began to see the dynamics of the relationship. She talked about how her mother was more concerned about the way things looked to others than about the reality of how things felt to the individual.

As Elaine began to explore what she really wanted for herself, as opposed to what everybody told her she should have in life, she was more able to make decisions about changing her circumstances. She began to experiment with more imaginative approaches in her artistic work, and she met a new partner with whom she was able to share and express her feelings and her spiritual journey. Her mother had great difficulties understanding this new-found change of course in her daughter, but Elaine was finally able to define her own set of values and stand firm.

Elaine's dream death in this case was more to do with 'giving up' than 'letting go', and she was able to recognize within the dream that 'giving up' was not the answer. She needed to take hold of her will and resolve to live her life according to her own principles. It was only at the symbolic point of death in her dream that she was able to see clearly the pattern that had been established in her relationship with her mother. Death was still, therefore, a significant symbol for a new awakening and a new approach to her life and creativity.

So the theme of change and transformation is the real significance behind the image of death in our dreams. As one door closes, another opens, but there are some things that we need to discard before we can move through the new door to our future.

SUMMARY

- In order to make room for new awareness, we must be willing to let go of old and outworn attitudes, behaviour and values.

- Death is a process of transformation, and the death of a person in a dream should not be taken literally.

- Find out what that person (or creature) represents in your life and recognize which aspect of yourself may need to be relinquished or transformed in some way.

- The death of one cycle or dimension of life will also signal the birth of a new cycle. Because we do not know what the new cycle will bring, we may well be afraid of letting go of that which is familiar, but we are constantly being urged to embrace new growth as a necessary part of our urge towards wholeness.

- Sometimes we need to recognize when death may be symbolizing an urge to give up or give in, when we should really be turning round and facing some kind of challenge to wake up to life. In these cases we may dream of coming to our senses in some way or deciding to fight back. This kind of dream can be useful in galvanizing us into renewed action and greater resolve.

CHAPTER 17

Dream On ...

THE PURPOSE OF this book is to give you some basic ideas and exercises to help you decode your dreams. With active imagination and Gestalt you can, like Alice, step through the Looking Glass and participate in your own dream world again.

The analogy is interesting because it is as though we are visiting a foreign world in dreamtime, a world where a whole new language has to be learnt, if we are to communicate successfully. Paradoxically, however, we (our ego selves) are the real foreigners; the world we visit is where the roots of our essence lie, but we have been exiled for so long that we have difficulty letting go of our notions of logic, predictability and consistency – apparent laws that govern our apparent 'reality'. And yet the inner world is a fourth-dimensional world where, like the Wonderland of Alice, anything is possible and where characters and images will transform themselves as soon as you talk to them. Also, like Alice, you become transformed in the process.

In order to make sense of the diverse imagery and symbolism presented in our dreamtime, it is sometimes tempting to consult one of the many dream/symbol dictionaries that are available these days. But it is important to remember that your dream symbols are unique to you, the dreamer. There are no simple interpretive answers and, while dream dictionaries are very useful to refer to when no personal associations to the symbols are forthcoming, they are best used as a last resort; otherwise they can simply add to the temptation to rationalize the dream.

As with everything else in life, dream interpretation grows easier to understand with practice. However, even the most practised dream worker or therapist will tell you that certain dreams can be particularly enigmatic. The kind of holistic and lateral thinking that they demand can defy our complex rational mind. Our logic seeks straight lines, but it gets confused in this inner world of curves and convolutions. Very often, the answers we are looking for are right under our very noses, and sometimes it needs someone else to point out the obvious. As a gypsy once said to me, 'A ferret can't smell itself.'

This is why recounting a dream to someone else can be useful whenever you feel unable to ascribe meaningful associations to the symbolism. Somehow, the very act of recounting and releasing your dreams in this way seems to allow you to find a new perspective, expecially if the person who listens is able to produce a new line of questioning or to suggest symbol associations that may have eluded you previously. For these reasons, many people would benefit from setting up or joining a dream group where they can experience being the objective observer of other people's dreams as well as receiving feedback on their own dream material. These need careful structuring if they are to be effective. Paradoxically, the picture-show that may have only taken a couple of minutes of 'real' time to manifest may take up to an hour to decode. It is not a process that can be hurried, and not every person in a group will get their dreams dealt with in the allotted time. However, it is important to know when to listen, how to listen and when to offer insights. Even observation of how dreams reveal themselves to others can give us useful connections with our own material. A dream group is not a forum for would-be dream interpreters, however tempting that may be, but rather a vehicle for helping others in their self-reflection. Many books now offer guidelines for running a dream group, and I would suggest that a good one to start with is *Working with Dreams* by Montague Ullman and Nan Zimmerman (Aquarian Press, 1979). Some ideas for running a group using such a structure are outlined in the Appendix.

There are certain categories of dreams, such as precognitive dreams and lucid dreams, that are beyond the scope of this book.

Precognitive dreams are those in which the subject dreams about an event which subsequently emerges as a reality in the subject's waking life. The event may be connected with the dreamer concerned, or it may be directed towards some aspect of the world around them. However, it does not seem to be based on any apparent knowledge of the event beforehand, and therefore it is of a prophetic nature.

These dreams do not lend themselves easily to interpretation, because very often the meaning of the dream only becomes clear after the event, when it is more or less replicated. This is also the case when people have telepathic dreams – for instance, a person may share the same dream as their partner or pick up some information about another person without knowledge of this information beforehand. Such dreams come under the heading of extra-sensory perception, and they pose many questions about our abilities to access information that lies beyond our present understanding of time and space.

Lucid dreams are those in which the person is aware that he or she is dreaming whilst in the dream state. The dreamer may even think that he is awake, and then discover that he is still dreaming. Such dreams often feel quite realistic in content, and the dreamer may even be aware enough to make decisions about how he or she will affect or change the course of the dream. Lucid dreaming has been well researched by Celia Green (see *Lucid Dreams*, Oxford Institute of Psychophysical Research, 1968), who has spent many years studying this phenomenon. These kinds of dreams may be experienced by some of us at some time or another, but this book is aimed at understanding the kinds of dream that most of us have every night.

Finally, it must be realized how vital a part our dreams can play in the whole process of creativity and problem-solving. Many of the inventions that science and technology have given us have been spawned in the symbolic vessel of the dream. Dreams have also been the basis of inspiration for the works of many artists, poets and writers. It is probably true to say that all dreams are about problem-solving of one kind or another, but we forget how useful a resource they are. Once the process of listening to and recording our dreams has begun, then we can expect to open up the channel of communication to our unconscious and perhaps even influence the kind of dream information that we wish to receive.

This depends upon how important it is for us to have a particular issue or creative problem solved. If it is uppermost in our minds before we go to sleep, then it is more likely that the dream will incorporate the issue into its 'story' in such a way that we will be given a new perspective on it the next morning. This is particularly effective for writers who suffer from writer's block or artists who have temporarily lost their inspiration. Much depends, however, on our determination. I do not suggest that it is easy to programme a dream, but we can certainly influence the subconscious to work in our favour over time. The dream may not always give us an instant 'Eureka!', but it will most definitely show us what we may need to change in our behaviour or thought processes to enable us to achieve a satisfactory solution.

One thing we can be sure of: dreams will never leave us, because they are a vital part of our stream of consciousness. Above all, they are practical, informative, inspirational and healing. I hope this book will help you to begin your journey on this stream and encourage you to take advantage of this life-enriching gift.

Appendix: Working in a Dream Group

DREAMS HAVE BEEN shared with other family or tribal members throughout time. As part of the process of initiation, dreams have been incubated in temples and related to shamans, priests and gurus. The products of these dreams have offered potent healing and problem-solving information both for the dreamer and for the family, tribe or community of which the dreamer is a member.

To record your dreams is to set up an important relationship with yourself. Recorded dreams can be worked on by an individual alone, although it may not always be easy to crack the code of your own unconscious immediately. The meanings of some dreams may be very apparent, but others may be hiding information about our feelings and behaviour that we do not really want to acknowledge. Often we need an objective observer as a mirror to reflect to us those aspects of our dreams that we are still denying to ourselves. The information that we manage to repress through the dream symbolism does not necessarily have to be threatening or unpleasant. Sometimes we have a hard time accepting positive changes and information that would bring more freedom and pleasure into our lives; often the rut that we are in, be it mental, emotional or spiritual, is at least a familiar one. New and more positive avenues of expression are not always easily assimilated.

Sharing a dream with a partner, family member or friend can create feelings of trust and closeness, but not everyone who is close to us is on our wavelength or willing to explore or even accept the relevance of dreams. If it is difficult for you to find an interested listener for your dreams then it might be worth considering either starting or joining a dream group.

Ideally, dream groups should only contain a small number of people. Depending on its length, a single dream can take up to an hour to work on; so I would recommend that, if the group decides to meet for two to three hours in an evening or afternoon, then there should be a maximum of eight people. That way nobody will have to wait for more than a couple of sessions before their dream is discussed. How often you meet, and your degree of commitment to supporting the group process must be established at the outset. You might, for instance, hold fortnightly meetings over three months, and then assess the results at the end of the time to see if the members of the group have benefited from the work and enjoyed the experience. The arrangement can then be renewed if the members so wish.

Sharing our dreams with others can be a daunting process. We might be afraid that others will judge us, as our dreams are products of our deepest inner sanctum and we need to trust our fellow members to be mindful of our vulnerability in exposing this level of our being. It must be stressed, therefore, that members of the group are not there to make judgements or predictions. They are there to offer observations, to ask appropriate information-seeking questions and to suggest associations. The owner of the dream, on the other hand, should not feel under any pressure to reveal any information that he or she feels unwilling to reveal. Equally, no person should be forced into offering a dream against their will. Information revealed within the dream group must remain confidential.

Guidelines need to be set for the structure of meetings so that precious time is not wasted in aimless chit-chat. For this reason, it is useful to appoint a leader who can decide when to move on to the next stage of the process. This presupposes that the group has a format in mind; the one offered below is one that I have used successfully and it is based on the pattern established by Montague Ullman (see p.128).

Ullman, disappointed by dream interpretation along Freudian lines which he had formerly practised, wanted to experiment with the use of dream work in group therapy. Conscious as he was that dreams would often be a vehicle for a lot of suppressed emotional energy, he wanted a method that would not be intimidating to the dreamer who was revealing such delicate material. He found a way that enabled group members to describe their feelings about the dream as if they were watching a film; thus the dreamer would receive a number of commentaries from which he could select those that felt significant to his own life experience. This method did not necessitate the dreamer baring his psyche to the other members if he was not ready to do so, but he was still offered insights into his emotional blocks which he could reflect on at his leisure.

There are three stages to this process, as follows. (NB: the leader or facilitator can also offer his or her observations as part of the group.)

Stage I

(1) The facilitator asks if anyone in the group wants to share a dream, preferably not a long one so that there will be time for one or two other members to work on their dreams later. It is best if a recent dream is offered, as its context will still be clear.

(2) When a dream is selected, the dreamer reads it out and the other members record notes with as much detail as possible. Any comments, excuses or criticisms of the dream by the dreamer are also observed, as these may be unconscious clues to emotional content.

(3) When the dreamer has finished, the members of the group are allowed to ask any questions about details that they may have missed. However, there is no attempt at interpretation at this stage.

Stage II

(1) Now the dreamer can relax and take notes as the other members make their commentaries.

(2) Each member is asked to respond to the dream as if it were their own, and to relate how it made them feel as they listened to it.

In other words, how did the dream affect you? (Refrain from making any objective comments about the dreamer here – this is a very subjective exercise.)

(3) Now the members are allowed to make their associations with the images as if it were their own dream, for instance, what feelings, tensions, aspirations and so on do the images evoke? It does not matter if some of these responses do not 'fit' for the dreamer; the dreamer will be able to absorb what is relevant. Again, this is not about interpretation or views about the dreamer or their dream. Neither does the dreamer have to acknowledge or respond to the associations.

Stage III

(1) At this point the dreamer is brought back into the discussion to respond to any of the information that might be of relevance to his life.

(2) He is also asked to describe his own feelings and ideas about his dream, and to link them up with recent events in his life.

(3) The group can then dialogue with the dreamer and seek further elaboration of material or ask further questions about the imagery. However these questions must be aimed at stimulating the dreamer to make new connections, and not to put the dreamer under any pressure to reveal more than he feels comfortable about handling.

(4) It is important to remember that some of the suggestions or associations that the group make will be projections from their own life experiences, and it is entirely up to the dreamer to select what is appropriate for him.

(5) Finally, the group leader needs to sense when a satisfactory conclusion has been reached in the process – that is, when the dreamer has gathered enough useful information to enable him to

continue his dream analysis privately and with some confidence at a later date. The leader must also decide whether there is sufficient time left to tackle another dream from the group.

This, then, is a suggested structure for a dream group. After a while, the group should be able to relax into a pattern and trust will be built up as members share their material in a non-judgemental setting. You will also find that attending a group will work wonders for stimulating the psyche to produce plenty more material.

Further Reading

ARTEMIDORUS, *The Oneirocritica*, tr. Robert J. White
(Noyes Press, New Jersey, 1975)

BRADSHAW, John, *Bradshaw On: The Family,*
(Health Communications Inc., 1988)

FREUD, Sigmund, *The Interpretation of Dreams*
(Vol. IV of the Standard Edition of the *Complete Psychological
Works*, Hogarth Press, 1953–74)

GREEN, Celia, *Lucid Dreams,*
(Oxford Institute of Psychophysical Research, 1968)

HAY, Louise L., *You Can Heal Your Life,*
(Eden Grove Editions, 1988)

JUNG, Carl G., *Man and His Symbols,* (Aldus, 1964)

JUNG, Carl G., *Memories, Dreams, Reflections,* (Fontana, 1963)

LOWEN, Alexander, *Bioenergetics,* (Penguin Books, 1975)

MINDELL, Arnold, *Dreambody,* (Routledge and Kegan Paul, 1982)

PERLS, Frederick S., *Gestalt Therapy Verbatim,*
(Real People Press, Utah, 1969)

ULLMAN, Montague and ZIMMERMAN, Nan, *Working With
Dreams,* (Aquarian Press, 1979)

Index

S

self, instinctual
  needing acknowledgement
    of 122
  and animals 42–3
  and Shadow 59, 88
Senoi Indians 30
settings 38, 59
  countryside 39
  house 38
  nature 42
  transport 39
Shadow 85–90
  transformation of 87
    and death 121
    times of 113
Shakespeare, William 23
sleep patterns 17–20
snakes 42
symbols
  and dictionaries 127
  transformative 81
  unlocking meaning of 57

T

techniques, interaction 57–63,
    65–71
temperament types 47
  air 48
  earth 48
  fiery 47
  water 48

temples
  dream 21
  incubation 21
timing 81
  and birth 113
transport
  bicycle 41
  car 41, 58–61, 93
  motor-bike 65–8
  public 41

U

Ullman, Montague 128, 134

W

walking 41
water 47, 51, 52, 56
weather 15
  see also elements
writing
  about dreams 33–4, 109
  inspired by dreams 129

Y

Yahweh 21

Z

Zimmerman, Nan 128
Zulus 29